DON'T ASK ME WHY
60 years a woman minister

The autobiography of

KATHLEEN HENDRY

ISBN 085346 1252

Published 1991 by
The United Reformed Church in the United Kingdom
86 Tavistock Place, London WC1H 9RT

Typeset & Printed by The Witney Press Ltd
Unit 1, Avenue One, Station Lane Industrial Estate,
Witney, Oxon OX8 6XZ Tel: (0993) 703981.

To my family

A commendation

It was probably at about the time she retired that I first encouraged Kathleen Hendry to tell her story in a book. I have nagged her once or twice since!

My deep conviction was that Kathleen could make a major contribution to the continuing story of women in the ministry of Word and Sacraments with our Church. In the 1990s we need a personal and historical perspective on what has been achieved and what remains to be achieved if the contribution of women in ministry is to be allowed its full place.

The reader must form his or her own opinion. I am convinced that we have here a valuable and perceptive account of one person's journey from becoming 'one of Grieve's men' at the Lancashire College in 1925 to being accepted as one of the country's church leaders at Birmingham in 1972 – although even then she was still part of a small minority of women. Perhaps a more significant part of the story concerns the way in which, in the following decade, Kathleen established the ordained ministry of women firmly in the minds and hearts of a large local church which had previously looked for 'good men' as its ministers.

There is a danger that some may think that this book proves that women are now fully accepted in our ministry. I do not believe this to be the case, nor does the author. What *has* been proved is that which should be obvious to the Christian Church – that God does not make distinctions of gender when he calls, nor distinctions of age or colour (Galatians 3:28); but it has been proved in situations where women have been 'special' and 'unusual'. The pioneers have done their work and those who walk the next part of the journey should derive hope from what has been achieved. That journey is towards the day when women's ministry is accepted as being as normal as men's. In some senses it may be every bit as difficult as the first part.

That is a comment on the situation in our own Church. It may be further complicated by the continuing debate in the Church of England, and in the Roman Catholic and Orthodox Churches. And I notice a worrying tendency in the Evangelical parts of many Churches to raise, on biblical grounds, doubts about women in ministry. We shall need to continue to engage in a biblical and theological debate which presents a contrary point of view on the ecumenical scene.

For me there are two extra bonuses in this book. The first follows from what I have just written. Kathleen Hendry has given us a book about pastoral ministry, about the joys and sorrows of being able to echo Ezekiel's words, 'I could sit where my people sat'. As she celebrates the diamond jubilee of her ordination Kathleen can look at ministry from a long perspective. What may have seemed trivial or frustrating at the time can now be seen as part of the gracious providing and purpose of God. Ministry can enable God to be found in the smallness of much human life. Arthur Macarthur's comment is more profound than most of what is said at the breakfast table – 'Kathleen isn't a lady, she's one of our ministers! And what a privilege that is!

The second bonus is that this is a testament of faith. Very early in the book Kathleen Hendry writes, 'I came into a world full of God'. As she has journeyed through that world, life has given her more than a fair share of tragedies and disappointments. She knows at first hand what suffering is. Yet she continues to witness to the goodness and mercy of God. It will be good if in the coming days, in her life and in these printed words, more of us can sense in our own experience the gracious love of the God and Father of our Lord Jesus Christ.

JOHN WALLER

Moderator of West Midlands Province of the United Reformed Church

Easter 1991

Don't ask me why

It was an important service at our church in Purley: an associate minister was being inducted. At the communion table stood the three ministers at the centre of the service – the chairman of Croydon District of the United Reformed Church who was presiding; the tutor in pastoral studies at Westminster College, Cambridge, who had preached the sermon; and the newly-inducted minister. All three were women.

As I looked at them from a front pew, I could not help thinking that I had been ordained and inducted before any of them was born. In the case of Jennifer Millington, the new associate minister, I had begun my ministry 30 years before she was born.

For a long time there were not a great many of us. When I was inducted as associate minister in Purley in 1975 I was the church's first woman minister; now, 14 years on, Purley was accepting its third. Nobody in the 1989 congregation seemed to bat an eyelid at being led by this very able trio. How times have changed!

What is accepted in church takes longer in other places. One day soon after that induction service I went into a Croydon bank to cash a cheque. The young man behind the counter protested: 'This is not your cheque book.' Indignantly I said, 'I beg your pardon!' He pointed out that on the cheque above my signature the words 'Rev K M Hendry' were printed. 'This is your husband's book.' In 1989 he didn't know there were female ministers.

I started thinking about my own experience of ministry and of the tremendous changes of the 20th century outside and inside the Church. My immediate reaction was: It's a different world, but on further reflection I question that statement. Certainly material conditions have changed. When my father was a minister neither he nor his colleagues had a car – all his pastoral visits were done on foot or by tram. He had no phone – but then neither did most members of his churches. He had no filing cabinets, no card index system, no tapes, no slides, no film projector; no radio, no television or videotapes.

In the sanctuary there was no microphone nor any amplification. He had a magic lantern to illustrate missionary work overseas and a loudhailer for open air meetings. Manses had no central heating and in the winter the churches were frequently very cold. Work was mainly restricted to the local church and the Methodist circuit – I don't remember him being involved with many non-church committees.

Relations with other denominations were almost non-existent. I can remember his delight when one day the Roman Catholic priest stopped to speak and shook hands with him – a dissenter. There were no immediate racial tensions and no doubts about the need to go and make benighted heathen good Christians.

Perhaps sometimes presentday ministers wish phones had never been installed or committees multiplied, or Buddhists and Muslims and Hindus had not come to be neighbours and made ministry so much more complicated. But how grateful they must be for cars and computers and visual aids and word processors and many more sophisticated gadgets. How splendid too the development of relationships between churches, between young people internationally, and in dialogue with other faiths.

But is it a different world? Are people really different?

People's opinions and attitudes change in the course of a single century, and yet I find the Bible – both the Old and the New Testaments – as relevant as ever it was in the past. The Old Testament has a lot to say that is still relevant about justice and wealth in the book of Amos; man is still cut down to size in the drama and poetry of the book of Job; it would be difficult to excel Isaiah's vision of the mystery of the majesty of God. The story of David playing his harp to relieve the king's depression is a good illustration of early psychiatric treatment, and many of Jesus' acts of healing suggest holistic medicine.

On the other hand all the bad behaviour known today can be found in the tales of Goliath and Jezebel, Herod and Pilate and a host more. And just as basically the bible message is of a God of love creating and ruling his world, so today's Church proclaims the God whose love is unfailing still.

Don't ask me why God continues to take hold of unlikely people to share in his work, which is basically the same in every generation though set in varying conditions. All I can say is that I believe he took hold of me at a time when it seemed very odd indeed to most people for a girl to go into the ordained ministry in this country.

The Bible presents a devastating analysis of the human predicament as it was thousands of years ago and it does not give direct answers to modern problems thrown up by scientific discoveries; but because the Biblical writers relate human experience to God and insist that this is God's world the message speaks immediately to our condition. Jesus' story of the good Samaritan comes alive in all sorts of situations as does the tale of the understanding loving parent with a delinquent son; and the account of the entrepreneur who built up his grain stores has a lot to say to those who are blind to everything except the profit motive.

If there had been no Church I would never have learned the Bible's understanding of life. Because of it a teenage girl cheekily critical of the Church came to spend 60 years as an ordained minister. Don't ask me why.

Chapter I

A daughter - Deo Gratias?

It was on June 21 1906 that I arrived at the Wesleyan Methodist manse, Bearwood Road, Smethwick. The previous year the Liberal Party had swept to power. The British Empire dominated the world, the rich Edwardians enjoyed wealth and revelry according to the historian, taking their goodly heritage for granted and ignoring the gathering clouds of conflict. Within years the Foreign Secretary, Sir Edward Grey, was to prophesy: 'The lamps are going out all over Europe: we shall not see them lit again in our lifetime.'

On the day of my birth, so the story goes, a neighbour dashed into the manse to put a silver spoon in my mouth. And indeed it was my lucky day. I ought never to have happened. If there had been a contraceptive pill I wouldn't have been born – my mother had made a clumsy attempt to abort me. The questions of luck, randomness, purpose and 'a divinity that shapes our ends' I have never been able to resolve satisfactorily. However, my mother, who certainly believed in God, evidently settled down and accepted me as a gift from God which she with my father must love and nurture.

My mother was 37 two weeks after my birth: dark and beautiful, well educated and much-travelled, belonging to a family that proudly claimed Huguenot ancestry, she had married an impecunious young minister against the wishes of her sister and brothers. My father came from a wretched poverty-stricken home – he hadn't slept in a bed until he was 16 – because he had a feckless drunken father. When he was ten years old my father was sent to work in a cotton mill, and on Saturdays ran errands for a publican for a penny per week, which the landlord kept back until he gave him half-a-crown (12½p) after 30 weeks. He was rescued by a church which invited him in one Sunday evening as he sat on the doorstep. When he was 26 years old he went to Didsbury College, Manchester, to train for the ministry. There he proved a first class student, winning a prize for Hebrew.

After serving the probationary years usual in Methodist ministry, he went as junior minister to the circuit at Delph, near Oldham. At that time Delph was in the district of Saddleworth which was part of the West Riding of Yorkshire; and it was in the church there that he met my mother. Later the whole of his ministry, apart from three years in the Isle of Man, was spent in Lancashire towns not too far from Manchester.

I treasure his obituary notice in the minutes of the Wesleyan Methodist Conference 1931:

> *'John W Hall, born at Ashton-u-Lyne, December 2 1871. Some years later the family moved to Droylsden, where as a boy, he attended Moorside Sunday School. He was converted as a youth, and began with characteristic zeal to work for the Master in cottage meetings, Sunday School and pulpit. After training at Didsbury College, he took his first circuit in 1900 and for thirty years exercised a gracious and effective ministry. He had fine gifts, a breezy style and a quaint humour which, combined with a strong faith in Christ as Saviour and a passion for the salvation of men, gave him great power in the pulpit, and enabled him to lead many out of darkness into light. Next to his preaching, his chief interest was in the finding and training of men for the preaching and ministry of the word – a work in which he was singularly successful. He had a kindly heart and great sympathy with the poor and the struggling, of whom many remember him with gratitude and affection. The last year of his life was marked by much weakness and pain which he bore with wonderful courage and cheerfulness. He passed away in peace on January 8 1931, a gallant and loyal servant of Jesus Christ.'*

So from the beginning I learned to be a very poor relation in my mother's family, and to consider myself immensely better off than my father had ever been as a child. On reflection now, it seems incredible that I took so much for granted and thought my childhood was like every other child's of similar circumstances. In his quaint way my father sometimes would say God broke the mould when he made me. His own life was so extraordinary he must often have pondered on God's mysterious ways, as I have often done. One thing I realise now. I came into a world full of God.

All my life, except for 13 years of marriage, I have lived in a minister's house. Once a locum doctor came to stay in my house and was astonished to discover the routine of a minister's week. Previously I had taken it for granted – it was the only routine I knew – but I began to realise how very different life in a manse is from most people's experience. It must have needed tremendous adjustment for my mother to be a minister's wife. She was fortunate in having some personal income that enabled her to have a maid, to buy lovely clothes and have a grand piano, but she had to put up with furniture provided by the circuit and there were no more opportunities to go to Europe and America where she had a number of friends. Although she was considered 'delicate', as many Victorian young ladies were thought to be, my memories of her suggest that she was a very lively strong character. She was a stern disciplinarian but I can well remember she would bring out an enormous heavy album of sepia photographs of France and Italy and tell me about her visits to Paris, Venice, Rome and Florence. And how well she baked! Every week she made loads of jam tarts and apple turnovers and currant pastries, most of which she took or sent to families in need.

On Sunday mornings when I sat in the pew with her she always supplied gelatine lozenges to keep me quiet during the sermon – there was no 'junior church'. At the beginning of World War I, I was sent home from school to knit khaki mittens for a soldier – it meant working with four needles and I was only eight years old. I cried – and my mother did the ribbing for me. On the other hand I hated the way she would sit darning at my side while she made me practise scales on the piano in the unheated drawing room. She helped me with French and heard me say my multiplication tables and occasionally took me on shopping expeditions, but her physical frailty meant that my father took me out, mostly on Saturdays. I'm quite sure she never regretted changing her social status for her life as a minister's wife and even in times of illness her sense of humour survived. She decided that after her death my father should marry her best friend and told me 'Auntie Maggie' would look after me. When a colleague of my father's called during her last weeks and suggested praying with her she laughed, saying that when she had gone it would take God all his time to look after my father and me and my brother!

We moved to Douglas, Isle of Man, when I was one year old and there my brother was born, so at three I was sent to school with a teacher friend of my parents, who probably taught me in the kindergarten class of Douglas High School. My father's ministry in

Douglas was so successful that 50 years later when I went to preach at Finch Hill Congregational Church people queued to shake my hand because they remembered him. What a tribute to a short three-year ministry! At that time Wesleyan Methodist ministers moved every three years, so in 1910 we went to Bolton, Lancashire. Regularly we returned to Douglas for holidays, and the beauty of the island, its seascapes and glens, Laxey's water wheel and the electric railway up Snaefell – together with many Manx friends – gave me endless delight, and I always hated going back to dirty old Bolton. My mother's health was poor in Bolton, and my father took me on Saturdays to the market for ice cream. He would stop time and again to say 'Spell this' – the name of a commodity in the shop windows; 'Piccalilli' was one of his favourite tests.

Katie, our maid, had come with us from Douglas – she was one of a family of 16 plus an adopted child (one of her brothers became a Congregational minister). When my mother was ill Katie insisted that if I didn't behave well God would let my mother die and then I would have a wicked stepmother who would ill-treat me. I only half believed her, and later had a stepmother I adored. On Sunday evenings my brother, who would then be three or four, and I played Church. He was the congregation and sang the hymns and I the preacher until I fell off the pulpit stool and sprained my ankle. The dame's school was next to the manse and my only memory of it is envying two sisters who had beautiful curls, whereas my hair was thin and straggly even though I stood still whilst my mother brushed it with a whalebone brush 100 strokes every night.

We moved from Bolton to Moses Gate, just a few miles away, the year before World War I. Along with the Congregational minister's daughter and several neighbours' children, I went to another dame's school, until the Congregational minister took his daughter away and sent her to the nearby Congregational day school, whereupon my father decided that what was good enough for her was good enough for me. In that school many boys and girls went half time to work in the mills when they were 12. Most of them were poor and made fun of me with my French middle name. I tried to curry favour with them by giving them little presents. The headmaster terrified me and sometimes I still fancy I can hear his rasping voice and the swish of his cane. When the caretaker died and other children lined up to see him in his coffin, I took to my heels.

The Lancashire Territorials marched past the house and my

brother and I sat on the garden wall waving Union Jacks; but it wasn't long before I realised that war was a terrible disaster. One of my cousins was killed at Gallipoli, but an incident in my father's church made an indelible impression. Mrs Tyler was a widow, and her only son – the one breadwinner in the family – was killed. My father went to the house and told us when he came home how Mrs Tyler had sat at the kitchen table surrounded with sympathising neighbours. One of them had said, 'It's enough to finish your faith in God, this is' and Mrs Tyler had thumped the bare table with her fist and answered, 'Nay – nothing can do that.' I suspect this was the very first time I'd been made to see religion had to do with real experience.

Because of the war, the Wesleyans invited my father to stay another three years in the circuit as superintendent. He was very pleased – at ten I would then be able to go to Bolton School; but the Wesleyan Methodist Conference of 1916 vetoed his invitation and gave him the options of going to the Shetland Isles or to the Oldham Road Church, Manchester – he was too young to be a superintendent minister. We went to live in Manchester – in a Roman Catholic slum district where the police patrolled in twos and we children were never allowed to go out alone. We rode our tricycle round the large unfurnished attics – there wasn't a blade of grass or a park within two miles. Katie couldn't stand it and went back to the Isle of Man.

The church was in the doldrums and had asked leave to close: it was my father's task to build it up. The situation was daunting and depressing. Within half a mile on the same side of Oldham Road stood an Anglican Church and Oldham Road Congregational Church. Little did I think that one day I would preach there. Across the road from the manse stood the Bee Hive and the Angel pubs and my brother and I played at counting their customers and the ragged children left to wait outside.

The chief layman in my father's church was a Mr Pattrieoux who lived miles away and owned a tobacco factory in Cheetham Hill. On Saturday mornings my father took me and my brother through Red Bank and Angel Meadow to see 'Uncle Herbert' and watch the process of cigarette making and packaging. 'Uncle' would give us half a crown each. On these walks, where we saw lots of children barefoot and ill-clad, my father would say if it had not been for the church which had rescued him we could have been in similar condition to those children. On one occasion, en route to the tobacco factory he stopped and told my brother to give a little lad the sixpence he had in his pocket. Very reluctantly my brother held it out and the other boy snatched it and ran off. My brother sulked until Uncle produced the usual half-crown. On the way home my father pointed out again our good fortune, to which my brother answered, 'Shall we go again next Saturday, and I'll give another boy sixpence.'

The move to Manchester which was really a cruel blow to my parents proved a great blessing to me. I went to the Manchester High School for Girls where Miss Burstall, later Dr Sara, was headmistress. She was a champion of women's emancipation, with a dramatic prose style. In her book *Retrospect and Prospect*, she tells how 'on a spring morning in 1874 an ardent schoolgirl stood on Westminster Bridge to look at the sunset. The struggle for better education for women was then at a point of critical difficulty; there was intense enthusiasm, earnest hope, but no progress. The passionate hope of youth seethed within her; the beauty of that storied scene and that flaming sky stirred her soul to a burning indignation. She looked at the hospital building, then the new model of its type, and yes, she thought, there are women sufferers, women nurses, but no woman can be a doctor. Turning westward she saw between her and the crimson clouds a vast black hulk, Millbank prison, like some monstrous beast from the river slime. Women may be and are, she remembered, prisoners, but the august vocation of the Law for counsel, defence and judgment is forbidden to them. And then her gaze swept round to the Palace of Westminster – focus and symbol of national citizenship, the Houses of Parliament. Dreaming as schoolgirls will, of things beyond possibility, she said to herself, 'If only I could be a Member of Parliament! I might as well hope to fly.'

During Dr Burstall's lifetime she saw her dreams come true, and as one of her girls I shared in the astonishing changes of the early 20th century. Her influence on my life was immense – I can never repay the debt I owe to her and members of her staff.

There were 700 girls at Manchester High School for Girls in 1916 and I was one of the little Juniors in the immediate care of Miss F W Harrison – generally known as 'Fanny'. It was Miss Harrison who taught scripture, and contrary to modern practice made us learn quite a lot by heart. Among her favourite passages, which I have always been glad to remember, was Joshua 1:1-11, 'As I was with Moses so I will be with thee; I will not leave thee nor forsake thee. Only be strong and very courageous.' She insisted on our learning I Corinthians 13:1-7 – the beginning of Paul's 'hymn of love' – and Psalms 23 and 27. Is it really a bad thing to have such helpful verses firmly fixed in young minds? They have often proved useful to me, just as verses remembered from hymns have helped me in needy hours.

We didn't meet Miss Burstall often. Consequently when she stopped me on the stairs, a shy little new girl, to say 'Well, Kathleen my dear, how are you getting on?' I was astonished. It was part of her greatness that she knew the names of every one of her 700 girls, even the names of insignificant second-formers. Of course we made silly fun of her 'penny lectures' on good behaviour – and her hairstyle and red stockings. We rebelled against school uniform and dinners as well as school rules, but so much of that school experience has 'stuck'. It was Miss Burstall who decided I should learn Greek as well as Latin, neither of us guessing how useful it would prove later.

Gymnastics and games were great fun at school – music lessons and Religious Education weren't. The staff – mainly single women who spent most of their working lives in the school – were on the whole competent and caring. Had it not been for World War I they would probably have left to marry and have children of their own, but because of few changes the school had an atmosphere of strong stability. It was of course a fee-paying school, though some of us had scholarships and there was a certain amount of snobbery about the girls who came from 'working-class' backgrounds. On the other hand the school community included a number of Jewish girls, some Armenians, and one or two Germans. Schoolgirls can be cruelly perceptive of the inadequacies of mistresses, and those who were 'soft' or poor teachers must often have been unhappy. Oddly, I remember one who taught English – not my best subject, nor was she my favourite teacher. Eira Jupe was an unattractive woman to look at but she was not only well versed in Kinglake's *Eothen* (with its remarkable description of desert sand), Palgrave's *Golden Treasury*, Browning's *Men and Women*, Shakespeare's *Henry V* and *Julius Caesar*, but she had the ability to fix them in the mind of a teenage girl.

In my school years Manchester High School for Girls was in Dover Street near the University and then some of the surrounding streets were out of bounds. Now Manchester's red light area has moved further out of the city. At that time Marie Stopes and Bishop Barnes of Birmingham were just beginning to speak out about sex. Without knowing what we were talking about, walking to town after school we argued about birth control and contraception, which we daren't have mentioned at home.

Education has changed greatly in 50 years! Children no longer work half-time at 12 years old – though 13 and 14 year olds often do newspaper rounds for pocket money and share domestic chores in homes which in my day were staffed with servants. There were no grants in the old days, and now I marvel that my father on a meagre ministerial salary never even mentioned my earning money – which I never did till I was 25.

In 1922, having matriculated and moved into the Junior Sixth form, the question arose – what career did I intend to pursue? Earlier, I'd dreamed of going to India as a missionary doctor, pictures of the sub-continent in our *Chatterbox* annual had fascinated me and missionaries on furlough had fired my imagination. Our family doctor in Bolton had been a woman, so it didn't occur to me it might be difficult for a girl to qualify, but my mother had become painfully ill and her suffering put me off medicine. The word wasn't mentioned but I suspect she had cancer. She died the night after my 14th birthday. A few days earlier she had given me a watch for my birthday and had said, 'I don't mind what you do with your time so long as you use it well'.

How should grown-ups deal with a young teenager on the death of her mother? My father was so preoccupied with his own grief, I was left in the questionable care of the housekeeper. She had tied the door handle of my mother's room to the stair banister-rail by the time I wakened to hear the news which I'd expected. I was terrified – there were no chapels of rest. Later somebody thought it proper for me to see my mother in her coffin and kiss her icy unnatural face. I hated that experience. The funeral meant a long journey into the West Riding to Delph village where the main street was lined with workpeople from the family mill paying their last respects to 'Miss Julia'. She was buried in a simple grave next to a colossal granite monument to the memory of a more illustrious member of the family. Her epitaph was the simple true sentence from the New Testament, 'She hath done what she could'.

Was it her last words to me burning themselves into my mind that eventually led me in the direction of the ministry? I don't know. When she was ill, she would ask me to play and sing hymns for her – as she herself used to do on Sunday evenings with visitors round the piano. Invariably she would request her favourite –

Who fathoms the eternal thought?
Who talks of scheme and plan?

The Lord is God! He needeth not
The poor device of man.

I know not what the future hath
Of marvel or surprise,
Assured alone that life and death
His mercy underlies.

I know not where his islands lift
Their fronded palms in air.
I only know I cannot drift
Beyond his love and care.

I knew that was my mother's faith – she never actually talked about it, nor did I, but I knew it was real and mattered supremely to her. She was never given to sharing her spiritual experience as Wesleyans often did in weeknight meetings, and when a pious old gentleman once tried to talk to me about giving my heart to God I had run away and told my father, 'I've finished with your old pastyfaced Christianity', but my mother's favourite hymn had sunk deep into my heart and mind.

Chapter 2

A name on a notice board

What should I do with life? At 16 I didn't know. Miss Lister, the Classics mistress at school, was very keen for me to go to Oxford. I had a distinction in Greek in the matriculation certificate and a good credit in Latin and she was confident I'd get a state scholarship. It was most attractive to contemplate two more years at school then three at the university, but my father said, 'What are you going to do after that? Teach?' No – definitely not. What else was possible? He insisted he couldn't afford to let me enjoy myself at university unless I had some further purpose. A year after my mother's death he had married her best friend, a war widow with two little boys, which had made me tremendously happy, but that meant there were three boys younger than me to educate. I argued that if I had a state scholarship it wouldn't cost the family anything for me to go to Oxford. My father argued back that it would be wrong to use state funds for me to have a good time with no end in view, so if I didn't know what I wanted I could leave school and stay at home until I did! Teachers thought such a decision quite mad – the Head pleaded that I already had a scholarship, but my parent was adamant!

So at Christmas 1922 it was goodbye to Manchester High School for Girls and there followed 2½ years for me doing nothing much – an experience which has given me a great deal of sympathy for teenagers who don't know what they want. It was useless to protest. I didn't feel particularly angry – in fact I quite enjoyed idleness. Nothing much was demanded of me in the house – my stepmother and a resident maid coped with the chores. It was quite good fun to have singing lessons and be in the church choir. The Stamford Street Wesleyan Church, Ashton-under-Lyne, was a very pleasant meeting-place for young people and in those days

Ashton was a good place to live in. The manse was the nicest house we'd ever had, with a tennis court and orchard only minutes walk away from attractive shops and the hills. Manchester was a tram-ride away.

In that period my stepmother and I became close friends. She encouraged my music, being a very good pianist and contralto singer herself. We often went to the cinema together and sometimes had extra holidays in the Isle of Man. I wonder how long such an easy aimless existence could have gone on? Every Sunday dinnertime I stormed in criticism of the morning service. According to me the only decent preacher was my father — and I was so scathing about others that one day my father challenged me, 'D'you think you could do any better?' and with appalling arrogance I said 'Yes!'

The Wesleyan circuit in Ashton had a dearth of lay preachers and it was a considerable problem for the superintendent minister to make the quarterly plan. Pulpits had to be supplied by lay preachers, sometimes from other towns. Consequently my father had gathered a number of local young men and two young women to train as lay preachers. They met at the manse on Thursday evenings; so when I cheekily said 'Yes' I was told to go into the Thursday class and write a sermon. But I'd already had a go – one of my boy friends was training as a lay preacher and he had suggested I should write on the text 'Fear ye not, stand still and see the salvation of the Lord' (Exodus 14:13) so I promptly produced the script. On reading that naive little effort my father was convinced that God had called me to preach; and so began lay-preacher training, theoretical and practical. The first church to which I was sent was West End Wesleyan Mission, Ashton-under-Lyne.

In 1924, in accordance with Wesleyan practice we moved to Radcliffe - a far less attractive Lancashire town than Ashton; a less pleasant manse too. I hated leaving Ashton – the new place was so to speak at the bottom of a basin, with the Bridge Wesleyan Church at the lowest spot. The Guides needed a lieutenant so that gave me something to do, but how I missed my friends and the choir – and when was I going to have a proper career? Lay preaching was alright, but...! The Chairman of the District assured my father that very soon Wesleyans would have women ministers and if his daughter would do an external London BD, by the time she got it the door would be open and she could go right into the ministry. How wrong can one be? Forty years passed before the Methodists ordained a woman.

Because it gave me something to do I applied to London, got the necessary books and began studying with no great enthusiasm or expectations. Then a funny thing happened. It was April 1925. Walking through Radcliffe my father saw a church notice board announcing the anniversary services of the Radcliffe Congregational Church. 'The afternoon service at 2.30 pm will be conducted by Miss Margaret Hardy of Lancashire Independent College, Manchester.' Lancashire College? As a student at Didsbury College my father had played football against Lancashire College, Whalley Range. It was the theological college where Congregational ministers were trained, but Margaret Hardy was a woman's name: a woman in a men's theological college? That called for investigation, so my father called on a Congregational deacon. Yes, it was true – Margaret Hardy was the first woman theological student at Lancashire College; yes, Congregationalists had already ordained several women. Why not invite Margaret to Sunday tea?

That evening I was to take the service at the Bridge Wesleyan Church. Margaret would come and hear me. She sat near the front taking copious notes and later, putting her arm through mine, she said 'My dear, it simply is not done'. Did I squirm! Whatever criticism I had ever hurled against any other preacher, I got back in the next hour. I was furious – who did she think she was? In any case she was an old fuddy-duddy (at least 35!) and if being a woman minister meant being like her – to hell with the idea.

Not unused to my outbursts, my father told me not to be a fool. I didn't have to be like anybody else. I had to be myself. On her return to college, however, Margaret went straight to the Principal, Dr A J Grieve and must have told a very different story, because a note came by post on Monday afternoon asking me to go and see him on Tuesday. My father went with me – I was nearly 19. The outcome of that informal meeting was my transfer from the Wesleyan Church to Stand Independent Church under the ministry of the Revd Oliver Gregory; an entrance exam to Lancashire College and an interview in June with the college governors.

There were no district councils, no provincial committees, no assessment conferences - it is a wonder to me that the governors of the college under the stern chairmanship of the Revd TT James ever accepted me. I was naive, young and fragile-looking, but from first meeting Dr Grieve I knew that the one thing in life I wanted was to be a Congregational minister. Mr James, whose dark eyes under bristling eyebrows were positively scaring, said 'Miss Hall, what do you propose to do if we reject you?' I answered firmly 'Nothing'. 'What about teaching?' 'No!'

It was as clear as daylight now why my mother had said 'I don't mind what you do with your time' and why I had learnt Greek and Latin and voice production and church music. And how strange it was that the college secretary was the Revd Joseph Ferguson – the Congregational minister in Moses Gate who was a friend of my father and whose daughter Joan had gone to that dame school with me (sadly, the next month they were drowned in a swimming tragedy in Wales). In June 1925 one other woman was accepted at Lancashire College – Constance Clark, who became Margaret Hardy's life-long friend and colleague in Leeds.

Because I was so young it was unthinkable for me to live in digs and no woman student could possibly live under the same roof as 40 men – therefore I had to sleep at home and travel daily. The three women had to share one study, partly because I wasn't in much. Having the necessary qualifications I was entered for the Ordinary Arts BA course at the university. I picked up many old school friends in the Women's Union, which was a very good thing because we three women were not allowed to be members of 'the house' in the college, although we were allowed to go to the Literary & Debating Society on Friday evenings. Today the college accepts students with O and A Levels and for some provides tuition in the first year to enable them to enrol for a university course. In 1925 a Northern Matriculation Certificate with one distinction and five credits was recognised as a qualification for entry to a degree course, although Higher School Certificates gained after matriculation were more usual.

It would be impossible to overestimate the value of Mr Gregory's ministry to me at Stand Independent Church and the kindness I received there during college years. How did it happen that I joined the only Congregational church in the country where there were people whose family I had known from childhood? At the Manchester High School and through all the years since, Nellie Pickstone, an Anglican, has been my great friend. Her father's relatives were 'pillars' of Stand Independent Church, and when I was not preaching away, every Sunday I went to tea to one or other of her cousins. It was a tremendous boon to an ex-Methodist stranger coming into a new congregation alone – having left my family at the Wesleyan church at the bottom of the hill.

Mr Gregory was a splendid preacher and the standard of worship, including the music, was very high. To me it was marvellous to listen consistently to someone who had such shrewd insight into the scriptures and such excellence of expression. It would be very wrong to criticise the faithful voluntary service of many Methodist lay preachers. I have often thought they frequently go unthanked and unappreciated. Today a large proportion of United Reformed as well as Methodist churches would not be able to staff their pulpits without them; but when I was growing up I sorely needed the highly professional ministry of Mr Gregory, for whom I am profoundly grateful.

Don't ask me why things fell into place for me as they did in 1925. The facts are: my father read a Church notice board, Margaret Hardy spoke to Dr Grieve, he sent for me, I found Stand church and became a student at Lancashire College all in a matter of weeks, after I'd been idling, doing nothing much for two years; and from that time till now – 60 years later – I have thought it not only right, but normal for me to be a minister.

There are many records in and outside the Bible of people being reluctant to accept the call of God. Having resisted pious appals and having scathingly criticised the Church, at 19 I was absolutely convinced a minister I would be, and began to think that all through life there had been indications and preparation for such a destiny. There was nothing dramatic or sensational in the experience: I didn't think I was fighting a crusade for equal rights for women in the ministry of the Christian Church – I doubt whether I was sufficiently altruistic to do so. I can only say that I was drawn into the work of the Church. One former teacher wrote to me – 'Who told you you have something special to say to the world?' That wasn't the way I saw myself. I simply knew that the one thing I wanted to be was a minister.

To myself I seemed an ordinary university student who thoroughly enjoyed the opportunities of college life. With amazing naivety I was not daunted by the difficulties a woman had to face in a man's world; the fact is I was blind to them. I wasn't scared by the warning that at the end of six years training I might not get a job – I was sure something would happen that would be alright. You could say I had an unbelievably simple faith, or that I was ridiculously young, or incurably optimistic – as my stepmother had thought when she first knew me and I had bounced in front of her with a butterfly net and announced I was going to look for butterflies in the maze of streets in Newton Heath, Manchester.

My father believed there is no more desirable work in the world than being a Christian minister and I would agree; if the clock could be turned back and I could choose again I would opt again to be a minister in pastoral charge. When people talk about the guidance of the Holy Spirit I surrender to none in my faith that God took hold of me and shaped life for me. I realise that such a statement exposes me to all sorts of criticism: I have no right to think I'm special; don't we all say God has no favourites? It is intolerable to claim God's care and protection for oneself in a world where so many lack life's necessities and suffer awful tragedies. The hazards in life are numberless – if my mother had known about 'the pill' I would never have been me – and yet very humbly I have to say I have known a mysterious dimension which I can only describe as divine. The more I think back the more amazed I am, first at my father's vision of me as a minister, and secondly at my own unshakeable conviction that it has been right for me to be a Christian minister.

There are those still who believe equally firmly that God cannot possibly intend women to be Christian 'priests'. I have no argument with which to counter their stand, I can only write about my personal experience. The word 'priest' has different connotations from the word 'minister' and I have long suspected that the objections some Anglicans have against ordained women could be equally applied to ordained men in the non-established Churches. I have never found a man colleague who has described himself as a 'priest' although we nonconformists often speak of the ministry of the Word and Sacraments. Is there a deep theological difference of emphasis in our understanding of ordination? I don't consider myself an academic theologian.

Three years ago I was invited by the Old Girls' Association of my old school to speak to its members on my experience as a woman minister of religion. Before the meeting began the chairman introduced me to an Old Girl who was married to an Anglican vicar. 'How d'you do,' she said, 'I've come to hear the other side!' Thinking to be friendly, I replied, 'Maybe we shall find we are on the same side.' Tartly she answered, 'I think not – my husband is a friend of the Bishop of London.'

I have both listened to and read the convictions of Dr Graham Leonard, the former Bishop of London, concerning the ordination of women. His understanding of the male 'begetter' and the female 'conceiver' I think I understand. The fact that Jesus came into the world as a man uniquely representing God cannot be denied, but what I cannot accept is the belief that in the process of human procreation the part played by one partner is superior to the other.

Why is it more wonderful to beget than to conceive – and who can prove it? I have known the ecstasy, mystery and the pain shared in producing a baby which my husband and I recognised as a gift of God. I also remember the woman who brought her little son to me to be baptised and said pointing to him in the pram, 'That's what drink does for you.' She had no illusions about the superiority of men!

I have never understood how Anglicans hold their belief in the apostolic succession, which seems to exclude from ordination nonconformist men as well as women, but I'm prejudiced, having come from a long line of nonconformists. Is it possible that today Anglican male priests recognise nonconformist men ministers as their equals? I'm not sure.

Again, if the idea of God as exclusively male persists, doesn't this make him too small? None of us can understand 'the high and lofty One who inhabits eternity, whose name is holy' (Isaiah 57:15). Our minds are earthbound, and the only language we know is the language of this planet. Maleness is only half of human personality, and I think for God to be real he must somehow be total personality, which is beyond my thought and language. It is easier for me to say God is unfailing love.

CHAPTER 3

College doors, and doorsteps

The college motto was εις εργον διακονιας – 'to the work of the ministry' – and it expresses the purpose of the old Lancashire Independent College, which stood at the end of a tree-lined road in the residential suburb of Whalley Range, Manchester. The Bishop of Manchester then lived in a big house in that road. The neighbourhood is much less salubrious now and the college building (often described as having a Queen Anne front and a Mary Ann back) with its wedding cake tower now belongs to one of the big trade unions.

Asked how many students he had, Dr Grieve once replied, 'About one in ten'. It was a great privilege to be described as one of 'Grieve's men'. By the charter of Manchester University the Faculty of Theology has no denominational bias, with the result that Anglicans, Roman Catholics, Unitarians, Methodists and Congregationalists were on the staff there when I was a student. With such a history it is scarcely surprising that in recent years Manchester has played a leading role in the development of ecumenical courses in theological education.

It was, and is, the practice for students from various theological colleges to attend university lectures to gain both Arts and Theological degrees. Naturally a girl student was not an oddity in 1925 in the Faculty of Arts, but the lecturer in Logic and the History of Philosophy did not take kindly to having one girl in his class. Nor did he seem pleased when I got a First in first year Logic – it didn't fit in with his ideas about women. Third year Philosophy I found difficult, especially as he insisted on my sitting next to him in seminars when he would push his little beard my way, flinging questions directly at me, to the amusement of the men. Thinking I would fail the exam I plucked up courage and asked him what I needed to do to make sure I passed. I added that I knew he disliked having me in the class. I think he was taken aback by my accusation but he must have muttered some good advice because I scraped through the exam.

A Jewish professor taught Hebrew to a small group which included one of my old Jewish school friends. A Unitarian student and I nearly always had equal marks. The university offered a prize for Hebrew and two prizes for New Testament Greek. We calculated that in fairness the Unitarian would get the Hebrew prize and I the Junior Greek one. Much to everybody's surprise, two Hebrew prizes were awarded and I got the Junior Greek one as well. Dr Grieve gave the college a holiday as nobody had ever won two in a year. I think I was the first girl at the University to win all three when I got the Senior New Testament Greek prize the following year, but I was not the first to get a Manchester BD. It was an older Anglican woman who beat me to it, and I often think what a shame it was that she could not go on to be ordained in her Church.

During the long years since training I've listened on many occasions to students dissatisfied with college courses which they felt did not prepare them adequately for the ministry. After getting an Ordinary Arts degree, Dr Grieve persuaded me to do an MA alongside the BD course. That meant passing an extra exam in the fourth college year and writing a thesis whilst completing the BD syllabus in the 6th year. All went according to plan until that last year. The subject for my thesis was the monster Leviathan in the Old Testament – which involved a lot of fascinating research, particularly into Egyptology. During the Christmas vacation 1930, I was to go to the British Museum – but my father became ill and died in January 1931. The following June – for the first time ever – clever-clogs failed a university exam in New Testament studies and so had to leave college without a BD degree. I was able to retrieve it the following year but Leviathan sank without trace.

Have I regretted the time spent on those abstruse studies? Nobody in my first Church was impressed by Greek or Hebrew or Syriac. Nobody was interested then in comparative religion or Church history or the psychology of religion; but I loved those academic studies. It was probably very good for me that I learned what it felt like to fail. Now great stress is laid on fieldwork – practical training for the ministry – and I'm sure that is needed. I was lucky to have been brought up in a manse and to have spent many midnight hours talking with my father.

Sermon class in college was a gruelling experience. Once a year each student had to preach a sermon to the rest of their year and in front of the Principal. Sometimes he began his remarks by saying, 'Tonight I'm on the side of the angels'; but I can still see the first page of one of my sermons on which the dour but brilliant Dr Robert Mackintosh had blue-pencilled every word he deemed unnecessary.

On several Sundays every term we were sent to various churches in and around Manchester, which meant for me, living at home, catching a train soon after 6 am into Manchester and getting home around 10 pm. Mine were the first footprints across the snow to the station on a number of Sundays; but at least no church refused to have me. One day when Connie went to a church in the suburbs the deacons held a hasty meeting and decided that if they rejected her there could be no morning service, so she might be allowed to take it from the floor – certainly not from the pulpit. At dinnertime they sent her back to college to ask Dr Grieve to send a man in the evening.

At Windermere one Saturday evening the deacons expressed anxiety as to whether I was old enough and competent enough to conduct the Communion service, but being assured that a previous visiting student was a year younger, they accepted me. It was at Wigan where a deacon took me home for dinner and his wife, on hearing my voice as we entered the house, exclaimed from the kitchen, 'Good God! The student's brought 'is girl'. Presumably three chops would hardly do for four people!

It is more than 60 years ago that the Jewish tutor teaching me Hebrew pointed out with a twinkle in his eye that in Genesis the Hebrew word for man should be understood as 'man embracing woman'. In the United Reformed Church today the ordination of women is not in question. The records suggest that the Congregationalists ordained at least one woman in 1917 and although Dr Maude Royden was not ordained she served as a minister and preacher when I was a schoolgirl.

Speaking with younger women ministers today I gather that they feel pressures at least as heavy as any opposition I ever felt. The new freedom they have gained brings new problems. I and my teacher friends in the '30s were required to resign on marriage – pregnancy was strictly a private family matter. Today the Church is more involved because there are guidelines for women who wish to continue to work during pregnancy and this obviously is a different situation. From the beginning of women's ministry in the Church stipends for women, as far as I know, have never been less than equal with men's remuneration. That was not the case for many years in the teaching profession. Tax inequalities between the sexes in the matter of domestic help and probably in other matters continue, and I can well understand that, now everybody is more aware of their rights, women ministers feel there are still battles to be won.

Whilst I was in college my father had moved, in the course of his ministry, from Radcliffe to Heywood and in 1930 to Oswaldtwistle, where after only four months he died. I never liked living in Heywood although the Congregational church there gave me a friendly welcome on my occasional visits. But it happened that the Methodist manse was situated near the homes of several university students – a girl and a boy doing medicine, a girl already a qualified dentist, the next-door daughter reading geography and one music student with a lovely contralto voice. They were all interesting travelling companions. From the male medical I learned quite a bit about foils and fencing and the building of a canoe! On Saturday mornings I chatted with three of the girls while we cleaned the house doorsteps.

At that time we had no domestic help and it was my job to get up first, clean two grates, light the kitchen fire and get breakfast for myself and brothers before catching the 8.30 am train – that meant early rising on Fridays when the kitchen grate had to be black-leaded! If I didn't like the town of Heywood at least there were good tennis courts nearby and delightful walks in Carr Wood and over to Owd Betts – and there was the village of Bamford with its lovely Congregational church. The minister, Mr Richards, and his family were good friends and I was given many opportunities to conduct services there and at Norden, for which Mr Richards also had responsibility. Such commitments reduced my visits to Stand and my friends the Pickstones but we never lost touch completely.

Towards the end of my college course, I was sent one Sunday as a supply to Shaw Congregational Church near Oldham. In the vestry a very smart middle-aged man said, 'Good morning, my name is Fred Platt, what's yours?' 'Kathleen Hall'. 'You're not Harold Mallalieu's niece are you? I go on holiday with your uncle!' Mrs Platt sat in the back pew and at the end of the service came down the aisle to say, 'You're Julia Mallalieu's daughter – you can't possibly be anybody else. I went to school with your mother!' Hospitality had been arranged for me at the local police station, but the Platts insisted I went to their house for tea. I just couldn't believe what I heard – as a young unmarried minister at Delph Wesleyan Church, four miles away, my father had lodged with old Granny Platt and I had always been taken to see her when visiting my aunt in Delph.

That Sunday I raced home to tell the story of the day. Of course my father was delighted – he also knew Mrs Platt's family in Shaw, the Taylors of the Wesleyan Church. Still more unexpectedly, the Shaw minister announced that he was moving to Leeds, and on the first Sunday of the vacancy I was again sent to Shaw. My uncle commented, 'If Fred Platt wants you to be minister at Shaw, he'll get you' – they knew each other as highly successful businessmen! But was it likely a church mainly consisting of working-class people would go for a 25-year-old woman with no experience, when most churches wouldn't dream of having a woman to preach even occasionally? The deacons met and recommended that church meeting should invite me to preach 'with a view'. Mr Platt's gardener objected – he didn't believe in women in the ministry, and there may have been other dissentients.

Mr Platt asked me to meet him at the Midland Hotel, Manchester to discuss the matter. It's a miracle I ever got that call! The five-star Midland Hotel was as far out of my world as Buckingham Palace. I walked round it several times not daring to go inside and ask for Mr Platt, who had assumed I would walk straight into the Palm Court. I went back to college without lunch. He couldn't believe anyone could be so stupid – or nervous? – as I had been. Even so he and the Shaw church dared to take me on, on condition I stayed unmarried three years. The dissentient gardener – a good Congregationalist – wrote and told me he had voted against me but would bow to the will of the majority. From that day we became good friends.

The men in college weren't impressed – whoever had heard of Shaw?

Maybe it was alright for a girl but they hoped to go to better churches.

I was thrilled to have a call. The one shadow on the scene was that my father who had been so keen for me to be a minister had died before I got a call and was ordained. I'd like to think that somehow, somewhere in God's providence he knew that the dream had come true.

[illegible]

Chapter 4

A church begun by a woman

In the 19th century illegitimacy – especially for girls – was not only a misfortune but a social stigma, certainly among the 'lower' and 'middle' classes in England. The 20th century has brought revolutionary changes in thinking. One-parent families are commonplace and some women deliberately choose to have a child out of wedlock.

In my younger days it was a respectable misfortune to be a one-parent family if one parent died – I myself brought up two girls alone because my husband died early. But in 1832 when an unknown unfortunate – never having heard of birth control and unable to afford contraceptives even if they had been available – got pregnant unmarried she was doomed to be ostracised in a small town where respectable people held puritanical ideas about sex. In the little town of Shaw on the Lancashire side of the Pennine divide it happened in the year 1832 that a woman whom nobody seemed to know gave birth to a daughter whom she called Betty Hall.

The mother became a recluse shunned by neighbours. The daughter, after such an unpromising start to life, was named at the centenary meetings of the Congregational Union of England and Wales in 1931 among the great men and women who had served Congregationalism with distinction during the last hundred years. It was she who founded, built and largely financed the church of which I became the first woman minister in 1931.

Strangely enough we both had the surname 'Hall' although our stories were so different. I had all the advantages of a good home, a privileged place in the Church because my father was a minister, and a first class education. She had the disadvantages of obscurity, poverty, and no education, but God took hold of her and used her in the service of the Church as surely as I believe he called me to follow in her church at Shaw.

The word 'shaw' is supposed to be derived from the word 'shay' meaning a wood; at least that was what the people of Shaw said – in fact it was almost treeless. Four miles from the then West Riding of Yorkshire, three from Rochdale, three from Oldham and about eleven from Manchester, Shaw once had the reputation for being the wealthiest little town in Lancashire. In 1931 there were about 30 cotton spinning mills – but they had fallen on evil days and very few people had escaped financial disaster. The glamour of the boom years after World War I had gone. The cotton trade had crashed and there was a great deal of poverty in the town.

In the 19th century industry had made great strides in the area – hand–looms had disappeared in favour of power-driven machinery in large factories. On wintry afternoons, viewed from Grains Bar near the Yorkshire border, those mills lit up looked like fairy palaces – which they certainly were not in 1931. But back in the 1860s industrial prosperity had also suffered a major setback because of the American Civil War. The distress of that period, when it was impossible to get raw materials from America, came to be known in Lancashire as the time of the Cotton Panic; and the suffering of Shaw folk then was intense.

Betty Hall was a factory lass, and because of exceptional financial ability she fared better than some in the disaster years. She realised that if her dependent mother and she herself were to survive she must get out of the factory, and one day she announced she had finished with the mill and was going to start a business in secondhand clothing and bedding.

By the time of the Cotton Panic, Betty Hall was already in her early 50s. However, as a middle-aged woman, usually clad in clogs and shawl with a handerkerchief tied round her head, in fair weather and foul she walked the 11 miles to Manchester, called at large suburban houses to buy discarded clothes and bedding, then trudged back to Shaw with them in a pack on her back. Other days she would carry her pack round the district of Shaw, climbing the rough moorland slopes to isolated dwellings to sell her goods cheaply to people who found secondhand clothes a boon in hard times. She must have walked more than 20 miles a day.

I suspect she would have revelled in jumble sales that now produce £300 to £800 in a couple of hours. She plied a hard trade, and made a fortune by the standards of her time. Her first responsibility was to provide food and shelter for her mother and herself but she made far more money than she ever needed for their simple comfort – and all of it went to Congregationalism.

According to old records there was a Congregational Church in Shaw in 1846 which was aided by the Lancashire Union but apparently failed and was eventually closed. The building was sold to the Primitive Methodists. It could well be that the Cotton Panic and its consequent economic pressures brought about the closure. For the next 20 years the few enthusiastic Congregationalists in Shaw walked to Hope Church, Oldham – Betty Hall among them. She had a dream of a local church and persuaded not only people in Shaw but leading Congregationalists in Oldham that such a vision could become a reality.

In 1885 she rented the Crompton Cooperative Hall in Market Street in Shaw for six months for Sunday worship and Sunday School. The first services were held on July 19 1885 when there was an encouraging response to the personal and poster invitations distributed. It was not till 1889 that the members drew up a constitution and it was decided that 'all *male* members be eligible for nomination to the diaconate'. The rule seems extraordinary in a church founded and built and largely financed by a woman, but apparently Betty Hall never held any office, other than Sunday school teacher. The fact did not prevent her exercising considerable power and being in the confidence of ministers and deacons till her death in 1913, when the Lancashire Congregational Union erected a simple granite cross to her memory in the local cemetery inscribed with the words 'She hath loved the habitation of thy house'. No epitaph could have been more fitting: her passion for her church, her love of its worship and service, her concern for its financial security was all-embracing. It is said that she only had two books – the Bible and Josephus – both of which she would read by candlelight in the evening.

I suspect that it was not so much the fact of her illegitimacy as the prevailing attitude of male superiority that prevented the church from electing Betty Hall to the diaconate. She would have made a splendid church treasurer. She knew and understood money far better than many male executives in the late 20th century – but how many churches today entrust their money to female treasurers, although the year book names dozens of women secretaries?

In 1897 the old corrugated iron building, first known as Betty Hall's Iron Chapel and later used as a Sunday school after she had succeeded in getting a church built alongside it, caught fire and everything in it was destroyed. It was the week of the annual Whit

Friday Procession so, without the new banner that had been burned, Betty led the procession armed with collecting bags, and it wasn't long before it was possible to build a new school. She was dauntless, and when I went to Shaw in 1931 there were a number of people who still remembered her powerful personality and her spartan way of living. Yet two other pictures of her came to light. When the foundation stones of the church were laid Betty turned up in a splendid black silk gown with a rose pinned on the bodice; and on another occasion two church friends made an unexpected visit to her isolated cottage and, the door being open, found her kneeling on a chair praying aloud to her God. Beneath her sturdy exterior and her often crude financial dealings there beat a strong loving heart absolutely loyal and true. Perhaps it isn't surprising that the church she founded has stood up to 100 often difficult years with a great record of unbroken witness and service.

The Shaw church in 1931 had an attractive semi-detached manse at the top of the hill road on which the church stood five minutes' walk away. When my father died in the January of that year my stepmother was allowed to stay in the Oswaldtwistle manse until August, housekeeping for the locum sent in my father's place. What should she do next? The boys had left home by this time but the youngest needed a base for college vacations. She could join her widowed sister-in-law in Cheshire or she could come to Shaw with me. She chose Shaw, and that meant I could provide the house, which she could furnish. Nothing could have been more convenient and pleasant for me. It enabled me to devote all my time to learning how to be a minister; but, my stepmother had lost her husband and I my father.

Chapter 5

The best-paid person in church

On September 15 1931 my ordination took place in the presence of Dr A J Grieve, Principal of Lancashire Independent College, The Revd TT James, Moderator and Secretary of the Lancashire Congregational Union, and the Revd S H Stowell, minister of Greenacres Congregational Church, representing the Oldham Board, together with a goodly number of Shaw Congregationalists and personal friends. At that time many church members were out of work and on 'the means test', but they paid their young inexperienced minister £5 per week plus a house and rates. With one exception nobody in the church was earning as much – a skilled engineer got £3, a 'little piecer' in a cotton mill 29/-. In 1989 I don't know any church where the minister is better paid than anyone in the congregation.

There was no problem in gathering an audience for a fellowship hour on bleak Wednesday evenings – it was cheaper and more comfortable to go to a warm classroom in the Sunday school and pay twopence for tea and biscuits than to stay in a shabby, cold and probably damp house where there was no 'entertainment' except perhaps radio. The entire congregation lived within a three-mile radius of the church – and neither I nor any other ministerial colleagues had or really needed a car. Members of the congregation lived in the same streets and it was easy to do a number of pastoral visits without walking far round terraced houses without gardens, and of course everybody in the street knew if one had called at No 6 and not at No 16!

Many of the houses were very poor – it was the exceptional one that had indoor plumbing or hot water from a tap, but there were no slums in Shaw like those in Oldham where 14 people shared one room. Most of the Shaw houses were scrupulously clean and it was a disgrace not to wash the front door step and scrub the surrounding flagstones with 'donkey stone'. There was only one house from which I had a message saying that if I knocked at the door it would be slammed in my face. I didn't go there until the day came when the woman begged me to go, and later grumbled that I didn't call more frequently.

One day, looking for an address I knocked on a door and hesitantly asked, 'Does Mrs Daniels live here?' The man said, 'Yes – we're just waiting for the midwife.' Years later he told me, laughing, that without offering any help I fled. The child born that day in that humble little house grew to be our church organist. After being head boy at the local grammar school, he read history at the Queen's College, Oxford and continued in education as a senior executive officer.

Walking round Shaw I got to know some of the best people I've ever met. The Hornes were a diminutive couple who lived in a council bungalow after they left a squalid, damp terrace house. Mr Horne was out of work and looked after Mrs Horne. In 30 years I never saw her stand up. She was severely crippled with rheumatoid arthritis. He would bring her the utensils for baking or sewing and he did the shopping. They loved the teenagers who passed going to and from the secondary modern school and who called out 'Hello – shall we get your coal in? Do you want a loaf? We'll clear the snow from your path.' The Hornes thought teenagers splendid!

When they had been married 50 years they gave a party at the church. She dictated the menu, the Women's Guild did the catering and the St John Ambulance service carried the couple to and fro. Their daughter Margaret, married to a GI and living in Sacramento, was a source of great joy as she kept in touch with them regularly. After that golden wedding Mrs Horne told her doctor she hoped to live to be 100 and he said 'Whatever for?'

She was chairbound, she was poor and always had been. She would tell how her mother had paid a shilling to a rag-and-bone man for a white dress for her to go to church on Sermons Sunday, and how she herself had been paid 3/6 a week when she first worked in the mill. Church had given her happiness all the years. Many is the time at the end of a dreary day I called to see the Hornes, and later went home ashamed but heart-warmed.

There were other sturdy characters who rarely complained of their hard lot, whose loyal faith went into the building of the church fellowship. Like Betty Hall some of them were unique. There was Fred Mills, a British Israelite who assured me church unity was simple – 'let 'em all join *us*' – and there was the member of the Women's Guild who insisted on giving me a currant muffin for my tea while explaining that she 'allus baked after black-leading t'grate as it cleaned me 'ands'. By 1931 there were several families with three generations in the church.

In the second year of my ministry two tragedies shook the church. The 23-year-old Scoutmaster and church secretary, a bank clerk, returned from a World Scout Jamboree in Hungary with typhoid fever and after several weeks alone in an isolation ward he died. Apart from his parents I think I was his only visitor, and all the protection I had in the ward was a white coat taken from the peg on which I hung my own; but whether it was typhoid or scarlet fever or diphtheria or flu, I seemed to be immune to infection – and at that time there weren't even sulphonamides in use. The same year a 19-year-old girl died of septicaemia after giving birth to a baby boy; it had been a 'shotgun' wedding. Not only did the two deaths of young people make a profound impression on me but the truth is no girl in that church 'had to be married' until the war years 1939-1945. Looking through the baptismal records for the years of the Depression before World War II I found that in five years only one family had a baby – economics didn't encourage big families.

In college we had been well drilled in the conduct of baptismal services, so when I was asked to take my very first baptism on a Wednesday evening in church without a congregation I protested – only to be told there was no father and as the child was to be brought up as the youngest member of the grandparents' large family they wanted a quiet christening. I gave in; the boy grew up in the church very satisfactorily and it wasn't until he joined the RAMC that he learned the truth about his parentage. He was devastated to find everybody had lied to him and it was some time before he recovered. I suspect that kind of situation is less likely to arise these days.

If in college I had been preoccupied with academic subjects, in Shaw very quickly I had to learn to relate to 'real' life. The Crossleys lived in a tiny house that opened onto a main road. The first time I called, Mr Crossley brusquely told me his wife was in hospital 'with twins'. Mrs Crossley was a woman whose story was a tragedy. Before I met her she'd had an illegitimate boy Robert whom I got to know as an excellent teenager. Mr Crossley's first wife had died and he had literally given his two daughters away to kindly millworkers who brought them up without any legal arrangements. Then he had married again and I suspect Mrs Crossley accepted him hoping to gain some respectability.

They had a little girl, Mary, who was four when the twins arrived in September 1931. Mr Crossley never worked so they were always poor. In October one twin died. On my first Christmas Day as a minister after the joyful morning service I got a call to go to the Crossleys. Mary greeted me chanting 'baby dead, baby dead', and I was shown the tiny boy in a white shoe box. I walked the half mile home in drenching rain wondering what Christmas was about. A few years later Robert was killed in World War II, and the day I visited the family Mrs Crossley and Mary sat eating platefuls of chips while Mr Crossley sat at the end of the table tucking in to fillet steak, onions and chips. The scene made me so angry I didn't stay long, yet I never heard Mrs Crossley complain about anything.

She came regularly to church and contrived to give to church funds. Church friends and church worship gave her the only happiness she had to the end of her days, apart from her love for Robert and Mary. Two men ruined her life but I don't think she ever imagined women should have equal opportunities or even be persons with rights. Great emphasis is put on rights for women and on the caring ministry of the Church in this last decade of the 20th century; in Shaw the church was a deeply caring community in the depressed '30s.

At the end of my first year's ministry the deacons, delighted that weekly offerings had risen to £3 per Sunday, offered me an increase in salary of £25. I didn't need it, so asked if I might spend it by taking three little girls for a week's holiday. The church members who had children aged 10-11 could choose the three. They proved to be Lilian, whose mother had died of tuberculosis and whose father, out of work, had never recovered from being gassed in World War I; Margaret, the daughter of the Hornes, and Emily, whose people were Londoners who had come to Lancashire after World War I but were unemployed. All three were 11 years old. They had never seen the sea though we were only 50 miles from the coast; they had never been further than Manchester. I begged clothes for them from relatives and friends and arranged to take them by boat to Douglas, in the Isle of Man, to a boarding-house run by a member of my father's previous congregation. Questions of insurance in case of any emergency never crossed my mind! I just wanted to give three little girls a happy week. We got there safely enough - then they were all sick! They were not used to the good generous food they were served, 'jam butties' and chips being their staple diet. They got better and we had a good holiday.

Every worker in 'the caring professions' sooner or later meets his or her match. Mine was Mrs Bailey. I never knew anyone who had seen her up and dressed - day in day out, year in year out, she sat propped up in bed by the living-room window of the cottage where she was waited on hand and foot by her downtrodden daughter, for ever in disgrace as she had an illegitimate child. Foolishly, in my first year I told Mrs Bailey when I was going on holiday: I must leave my address in case she died. Then I learned she'd told my predecessor the same thing – the deacons said on no account was I to break my holiday. Years later, during my second term at Shaw the family sent in haste – Mrs Bailey was dying, the room was packed and in a loud voice Mrs Bailey was calling 'Lord take me! Lord have mercy! Lord take me! Our Annie, fetch me a glass of milk!'

Much later she sent for me to discuss her funeral: she must be taken into church and, after the burial, tea was to be served with the menu of ham and salad she then chose. One day Mrs Bailey actually died and the funeral arrangements were put in hand. As I met the bearers and coffin followed by the family at the church door I turned to walk down the left aisle of the church – there wasn't a centre aisle. Walking slowly, I began to recite the familiar words 'I am the resurrection and the life, saith the Lord' and as I moved forward I got a funny feeling that I was alone. On reaching the communion table an agitated undertaker caught up with me to whisper, 'She's too fat - we can't get her through the door'. So Mrs Bailey never did go to church all the 20 years I knew her.

But there was another side to being a minister – I never saw myself as a social worker. Sunday worship was a top priority. Morning congregations were sparse – a five-day working week was still some way off and after busy Saturdays 'a long lie in' on a Sunday morning was very attractive if not essential. There were two sessions of Sunday school at 9.30 am and 2 pm, but the adults came in large numbers at 6 pm. Social revolutions have changed the pattern of Sunday completely over 50 years. For most now Sunday morning provides the major act of worship. Sunday schools have given way to family church, often with creche facilities and better teaching.

In the old Sunday School I knew, there were literally hundreds of children whose parents only appeared on Anniversary Days to hear 'our Lizzie' sing a solo and at the annual procession when 'our

Johnny' carried the banner. There were some splendidly devoted teachers and in Shaw Mr Platt was one who must have influenced many lads for good during long years of service. Anniversary Sundays in the town had a strict time-table and woe betide any church which attempted to change its date and clash with a neighbouring congregation, because it was a matter of courtesy to support each other's special occasions.

On Whit Friday all the churches took to the streets in great processions headed by bands of varying quality and fame. It was regarded as an act of witness to walk with the church, and my church had some splendid processions with up to 100 Scouts, Cubs, Guides and Brownies supported by a May Queen and retinue and a crowd of grown-ups. Non-churchgoers lined the streets to see the displays and in Manchester Whit Monday and Whit Friday were completely dominated by the walks of the churches. Were those processions shows of strength, or weakness? Was there unworthy rivalry between the various churches? The years have seen their disappearance from most towns, but in times when there were fewer exciting occasions they were greatly enjoyed by many children and grown-ups. In the afternoon on Whit Fridays finery was changed for play clothes and sports and buns were pursued in fields, if the weather was kind, and in Sunday schools if it rained. These occasions, anniversaries and Whit walks were the highlights of the year, rather than the holy days of the Church calendar. On Good Friday people worked in the mills and in the nonconformist churches far less emphasis was laid on the celebration of Advent and Lent and Trinity Sundays than is now common practice. It surely is a great advance that we do follow the Church year together in all the Churches, and largely work with similar patterns of Christian education.

The story of Alice Reid is a curious one. I first knew her because her two little girls were sent to Sunday school. The father left Alice and took the children to live with the 'other woman' in Cheshire where he taught them to hate Alice. She was devastated and soon became one of the most notorious women in Shaw. She had some talent as a comedienne and when the Sunday school produced a pantomime one winter the producer brought Alice in as Mother Goose. I cringed to see her with 'my' girls on the stage. After the show there was a party and I had to present a whist prize to Alice. Later I sat down with her and to my amazement she told me how one of the children had asked her which church she attended. She said to me, 'You know me and what I am – do you believe in forgiveness?' I had to answer I couldn't be a minister if I didn't. She began coming to the evening service and eventually became a church member. So one day she was faced with the question, should she walk with the church in the Whit Friday procession? It would mean sniggers from her old pub companions who would be watching. Alice made her silent witness – she walked with the church. It's an incident I remember when I think about outreach. Years later, at a London committee the county secretary for women's work in Somerset told me Alice's elder daughter was living near her in Frome. We were able to effect a reconciliation with Alice. When the girl came to see her mother in Shaw, Alice, overwhelmed with joy, wept that God had answered her prayers.

Chapter 6

'A growing social concern'

It is now the accepted practice of the URC that young ministers have 'a father (or mother) in God' during the early years of their ministry to guide reading and to give friendly support and pastoral care. It wasn't so in 1931; but in Shaw I was tremendously fortunate in having a layman in the church who was a 'minister's man'. Fred Platt and some of his friends in other Oldham churches rendered invaluable service to many ministers.

In recent years it has seemed to me that our churches have lacked what I have called 'ministers' men', and I can't explain why. Nor has their place been taken by women! I have known a few women benefactors who have contributed large sums of money to the Church – and from my father's time on there have been some few women who have had fantasies about ministers. I have had the good fortune to be supported by several longstanding friends, but they are all women in the teaching profession who have not been members of my churches. I have feminist friends who object to the hymn 'Rise up, O men of God'; I sometimes wish they would – because they often leave the chores of the Church as well as praying and caring to women.

When Sunday's work was finished, Highfield, the Platts' home, was always open to the minister and his wife - and in my case to my stepmother. A sumptuous supper was served and any little problems that had cropped up were easily forgotten in that warm friendly home. I suspect I was not the only young minister who was liable to be self-critical on Sunday evenings and, being tired, exaggerated the value of trivial comments heard during the day, and it was good to be able to let off steam or just relax with understanding and loyal friends. During the week Fred Platt read the *Manchester Guardian* and always noted the book reviews. He bought me many theological works which I might have missed otherwise. As he was a magistrate and chairman of the children's court, he shared his concern for young people with me and on several occasions took me to see delinquents in approved schools. If there were local people in trouble he followed their cases up and where possible told me about them, so that I got insights into social conditions and people's behaviour that I would not have gained in the ordinary pastoral work of my church. (A habitual burglar who lived opposite to us sent his children to our Sunday school. When he had to appear in court he asked Mr Platt, chairman of the bench, if he would lend him a suit in which he could appear before him!)

There were not many men in the '30s who were as shrewd as Mr Platt in counselling a new minister. Always anxious that a very high standard should be maintained in worship, he insisted that one Sunday in every month I should preach away from Shaw, so that one week in four I should be spared from making two sermons and have time to read and at the same time have the opportunity of seeing other churches. At that time most churches tried popular services of one sort and another – Sportsmen's Sundays, Men's Sundays and above all Ladies' Days. On these occasions the idea was to have a ladies' choir, female organist, female stewards to take up the offering and especially a female in the pulpit. There weren't many female preachers to choose from – consequently invitations poured into my manse from a great variety of churches. Mr Platt advised me to turn them all down – it wasn't in the best interest of women in the ministry for me to have a reputation as a popular star on Ladies' Days – and how right he was. I took his advice and only accepted 'straight' invitations, eg for Harvest Festival or church and Sunday school anniversaries and arranged straight exchanges with men colleagues. His wisdom and generous friendship helped me incalculably in those early years.

In the first year of my ministry I was introduced to the Congregational May Meetings in London by Mr and Mrs Platt, who engaged a private suite at the Waldorf Hotel! After attending morning sessions in the (pre-war) City Temple, we went to theatre matinees and had evening parties at the Waldorf to which I invited friends. It was many years later that I learned to work so hard at the May Meetings, first as chairman of the Women's Committee and then as chairman of the Ministerial Training Committee, that there was scant opportunity for eating and sleeping and none for lavish entertainment!

Relationships between the churches in Shaw and in the Oldham

Congregational Board were good. The vicar of Shaw invited me more than once to preach in the parish church and he came to my church. The Methodist Church was the strongest nonconformist church locally and although members of the congregation were friendly, I got the feeling they considered me a 'deserter' - which I was!

After I married, a new vicar came to Shaw – an Anglo-Catholic who would not tolerate my successor David Smith, and would not share in a public service at which the Salvation Army band played. During his years at the parish church cooperation was virtually impossible, but seeds had been sown and the congregations continued in friendship.

By the standards of the 1980's – even in the North – most of my congregation were poverty-stricken but they rarely complained and, as I thought strangely, they always returned the Conservative candidate to the House of Commons. Dissidents said if you tied a blue ribbon to a pig in Shaw they'd vote for it – it was something I never understood.

One lovely June morning I was summoned to a house because Mrs Russell's husband had dropped dead. He lay there on the rag hearth-rug just 34 years old; he had been for a walk and was so underfed it had killed him. He had been earning 29/- per week to keep four. One Christmas Eve I called to see a family of seven who had a rabbit for Christmas dinner and little else. Ten shillings was thought to be a wonderful present. Miss Crossley was a chronic invalid – the walls of her tiny house were wet and the bed had to stand away from them in the only room with a handful of fire. She never had anything to eat on Thursday till tea-time when she got her weekly allowance. Every week her one pleasure was to put sixpence on the football pools and when one day the dream came true and she won £200, instead of spending it on herself and her rented house she doubled her freewill offering to the church. An 11-year-old won a scholarship to the local grammar school and her parents argued they couldn't possibly afford to send her. The church found support for them and she became a senior officer in the Inland Revenue service after a most successful school career.

The first suicide I ever saw was that of a deacon – thrown on the scrap-heap by the mill he had worked in, 'man and boy', for near 50 years. He drowned himself in the Coffin Lid Mill Lodge. Fifty years later his grandson, having made a distinguished career in the Civil Service, was awarded an OBE. The family – founder members – are still associated with the Shaw Church. It was much easier to minister to the people in Shaw then than it is to minister to those who have everything. They readily believed 'God is our refuge and strength – a very present help in time of trouble' but, as someone else has asked, 'What do you say to people who tell you everything in the garden is lovely?'

There have always been mixed motives for church attendance and there were men in Shaw who probably went to the Congregational church because Fred Platt was an employer – and maybe he could find a job for an out-of-work person. At a different social level, haven't others found it advantageous to belong to Rotary, or the golf club, and the Church of England? For the most part women could find work more easily than the men only skilled in cotton spinning. Women's labour was cheap: a domestic servant's wage was often less than £1 a week if she lived in. Of course there were no nurseries for children whose mothers worked; neighbours could earn a few shillings minding children before and after school hours and quite often there were grannies living nearby who would oblige.

The Shaw church's centenary booklet records that '1935 was an important year in the life of Shaw Congregational Church, being the Jubilee. A special service was held on Friday July 19 to commemorate the founding of the church and on October 26 a Jubilee Reunion took place in which former ministers took part. The Jubilee Anniversary services were conducted by the Revd Leyton Richards of Carrs Lane, Birmingham.'

Mr Richards was a personal friend of the Platts and he invited me to go and preach at Carrs Lane, with the result that he asked if I would consider the post of assistant there; but – was it conceit? – I enjoyed being in charge of my little church at Shaw. One of the projects for jubilee year was to improve the Sunday school building – there were no indoor toilets and very inadequate kitchen facilities in a classroom. The great asset was a large upstairs hall capable of seating 400 people, used regularly for all kinds of activities including dancing and Guides' and Scouts' games. On the ground floor there were a number of small classrooms separated by lath and plaster walls. An architect from Oldham – invited to make changes downstairs – discovered to our horror that the big floor upstairs was carried on half-inch joists. It was a miracle it hadn't crashed on many party occasions, as one in Liverpool had done about that time. The £500 so sacrificially raised for improvements had to go on putting in girders to carry the top floor and provide one loo.

Over the years, time and time again Shaw, intending to take three steps forward, has had to retreat two steps – the church building after the 'black-out' years of World War 2 has had several serious outbreaks of dry rot – but always the congregation has responded generously and refused to be defeated.

During the years 1935-38 there were 'ominous developments on the international stage and the influence of these can be detected in the evidence of a growing social concern in the church' to quote again from the centenary booklet. 'At a church meeting in March 1935 the minister spoke of a Parliamentary White Paper proposing large sums of money to be spent on armaments. There had recently been a peace ballot in the district and letters of protest were sent to the Government, the Parliamentary Member and the Press. In June that year a League of Nations Peace Campaign took place in Shaw, led by a group of Cambridge students. Various meetings were held and during that period the church was open from 8 am – 8 pm daily for prayer and meditation.' On reflection it seems that the people in Shaw then were more concerned with these wider issues than with their own low standard of living. I don't remember ever being involved with protests to the authorities about poverty. In the routine of the pastoral ministry neither my people nor I anticipated the approach of the Second World War – nor did I dream of change in my personal life.

Chapter 7

A life-changing visit to the doctor

Before the arrival of the National Health Service, in July 1948, very few people were able to have health insurance apart from manual workers; ministers and other professional people certainly were excluded from 'the panel'. But I never remember any doctor's bills coming to our family, and when I went to Shaw I was told that Dr Maitland would look after me. The staff of the four general practices had agreed among themselves to share the care of ministers and their families. I learned later they regarded such kindness as fire insurance! Dr Maitland was not a churchgoer, being much more interested in horses, but his wife was a deacon in my church. Before my time in Shaw he had his brother as partner in the practice, but Dr George had died and Dr Edward had continued with an assistant in the winter months and alone in the summer. Newly qualified doctors were not required to serve a year as trainees, so they sought posts in general practice or hospitals soon after they graduated.

In October 1934 a new assistant came to Dr Maitland, a Scot from Blantyre who quickly gained popularity in Shaw. Mrs Maitland told me how many girls in the town found they had minor ailments needing the attention of the new doctor. In the early summer of 1935 I had a bad attack of hayfever and made an appointment to see Dr Maitland at 4 pm at the end of his afternoon surgery. In the surgery there were two consulting rooms, a dispensary and a draughty corridor lined with bentwood chairs where patients waited for attention. There was no receptionist, no dispenser, no nurse and no appointment system. I was privileged to go at the end of the afternoon. The new Dr Hendry, having seen his last patient, came into the passage and asked if he could help me. With something very near disdain I replied I had an appointment with Dr Maitland. A few minutes later Dr Maitland called Dr Hendry from the dispensary to meet Miss Hall, the Congregational minister. So this was the good-looking young Scot I'd heard so much about! Months went by and I didn't see him again.

The following January at a production by the local musical society of which Mr Platt was president we met again. I had a very bad cold and jocularly Mr Platt suggested that Dr Hendry might prescribe for it. He would be delighted to do so if I would go to the surgery. I insisted that I didn't need the services of a doctor for a bad cold. The last week in February at that time was the occasion of a visit to the district of a deputation of London Missionary Society missionaries on furlough, and almost every year it snowed that week. On the Sunday local ministers moved around each other's churches, and after trudging home through the snow at dinnertime that year I had to admit my throat was bad, and I had the evening service to take at Shaw. So I rang the surgery. Yes, there was a Sunday afternoon surgery and Dr Hendry would be glad to see me. When I arrived he greeted me by saying, 'Have you read Stalky & Co? I gloat, I gloat, I gloat!'

So began the friendship which led to engagement and marriage. For several months we met secretly. I knew that if I married I would have to leave the ministry – even my teacher friends had to resign when they married. Consequently, when we announced our engagement on New Year's Day 1937 we faced questions and criticism. Hadn't I taken vows on my ordination that I was now breaking? Even my good friend Mr Platt said he always sacked his secretaries if they got engaged, as their minds were no longer on their work. Some church leaders accused me of letting the side down; hadn't the critics always said women in the ministry would pack up and get married? It might have been different if I were to marry another minister. But our love for each other was irresistible and we agreed together that if God still needed me as a minister in his Church the way would eventually open. Meanwhile we were both quite sure we belonged to each other.

Jim's father was an elder of the Church of Scotland in Blantyre, his mother was involved in church work, and his sister had married a son of the manse. His uncle was a Baptist minister of high repute in Airdrie, so they were not too shocked at the idea of having another minister in the family, and they were a delightful family. As Dr Maitland's assistant Jim was earning about £400 per year plus board and lodging, and in true Scots fashion he had to pay back to his parents the cost of his university education. So we couldn't plan to marry until April 1938. It would mean resigning from the ministry of Shaw church and it would also mean staying in the town.

My aunts and uncles in Delph thoroughly approved of Jim, as did Dr Grieve at college. He assured me that he was very glad to know I was to have a lifelong loving relationship and readily agreed to conduct the wedding service. I went to see the moderator, who insisted that I must drop my maiden name from the year book. Elsie Chamberlain was allowed to keep hers, but I have long been grateful that I changed to Kathleen Hendry. It was a tremendously happy period in spite of the niggling question about my defection from my calling. Was I making a great venture of faith or was I rationalising the situation? Only time would tell. The surgery had its own comment on our engagement. As two chronic regulars sat waiting for attention the one said to the other,"Ast 'eard 'bout yon mon? 'Ee's getten engaged – aye, an' its a bit of awreet. 'Ee brings 'em inter world an' 'er carries 'em out – an' they both geet paid.'

During my first seven years in Shaw I had for the most part avoided press publicity and the local newshounds hadn't been interested in my work; but as soon as I got engaged to a local doctor they were after me and were determined to be around on our wedding day. They turned up at least once on the wrong date, but eventually cornered a bridesmaid and gathered some details. I wished they'd been as diligent in seeking information about the church and its many activities.

We had amazing luck with a delightful house which had a smaller one next door which my stepmother was able to rent. She was very happy about my marriage and as I had no father I asked her to 'give me away', which she did with grace and dignity. In keeping with the tradition of the Hendry family the four bridesmaids wore white. As Jim was a Rover Scout, the Scouts provided a guard of honour. The second hymn we chose (by Henry Arnold Thomas) expressed our deepest feelings:

> O brother man for this we pray, Thou brother man and
>   sovereign Lord,
> That we Thy brethren day by day may follow Thee and
>   keep Thy word;
> That we may care as Thou has cared for sick and lame
>   and maimed and blind
> And freely share as Thou has shared in all the woe of

all mankind.
That ours may be the holy task to help and bless, to heal and save;
This is the privilege we ask and this the happiness we crave.
So in Thy mercy make us wise and lead us in the ways of love
Until at last our wondering eyes look on Thy glorious face above.

After lunch, followed by a tea dance, Jim and I escaped in the car which had been carefully hidden from Scots colleagues anxious to repay Jim for some earlier pranks, to Moffat and on to other Scottish retreats. When we got back Jim had a 50-50 partnership with Dr Maitland, which was an unusual and very advantageous arrangement.

On our return from holiday in the summer of 1939, Dr Maitland announced that he had been ill in our absence and advised that he could not survive another winter in Shaw, and so wished Jim to buy his share of the practice. I was pregnant, and in September war was declared. Jim was told how tremendously lucky he was to have control of a large practice at the age of 34, but he realised what very heavy responsibility was involved. Because of the war he could only get temporary help in the winter months and, whilst he was exempt from military service, for the most part he had no holidays and did two men's work. Shaw was considered a 'neutral' zone – too near to Manchester to be a reception area for evacuees but not sufficiently close to get much damage from the blitz on the city.

Our daughter Joyce was born in November 1939 and enjoyed all the luxurious baby things of pre-rationing days. She occupied my time except on Thursday afternoons and evenings when Ethel our maid took charge and Jim and I went out together. Ethel loved having responsibility for the baby once a week, and of course Granny next door was delighted to see her every day. The first year passed quietly and quickly. The church called the Revd David Smith to be its minister and he and his wife Mary became firm friends with us. He did a magnificent job of work, especially with the young people who were called to the armed services. Later Jim became one of his deacons and Scout Commissioner. David was the church Scoutmaster.

Nearly half my short married life was shadowed by World War II. For Jim and me those were very happy years in which our routine living was not severely disrupted. Our house furnishings and Joyce's baby things had all been purchased before rationing and 'utility' production. As in other places, of course, there were inconveniences like the black-out, restrictions in the use of petrol, food and clothes rationing. Before London had an air raid the only disused mill in Shaw got a direct hit, and much later a land-mine fell harmlessly in a field half a mile away. Our house had an unusual wash cellar with a huge fireplace where a coal fire burned warmly at night which served as an air raid shelter and held chairs and camp beds for ourselves and neighbours; but we got used to air raid warnings and often didn't bother to take the baby down to the cellar. Jim became accustomed to driving to emergency calls in the blackout, and because he had so many kind patients we were never short of farm produce and sugar and chocolate. I had no professional responsibilities; it was my successor David Smith who looked after those who were taken into the forces and their families.

World War II was unlike the trench warfare of World War I and church war memorials testify to fewer casualties in the services. Dresden and Coventry, London and many other cities and most of all Hiroshima and Nagasaki showed that warfare had really become the mass killing of civilian men, women and children. Two young women in the church at Shaw lost their husbands and each was left with a baby to bring up. Two of my relatives suffered poignant tragedies. A cousin, a squadron leader, having completed a stint of daring Pathfinder raids leading bombers to their targets, died in the RAF of appendicitis at Christmastime; and on the very last day of war in the Far East the husband of one of Jim's cousins was killed in Burma.

Jim, like me, had listened to the Revd Dick Shepherd and was a pacifist. As far as I can remember there was little or no jingoism in Shaw – lots of disgust and wry humour about Hitler and naturally wholehearted support for the war effort, together with willingness to look after refugees and evacuees. For some months we had living with us two ministers, man and wife, who had escaped from Germany and were sponsored by Bishop Bell of Chichester and later by the London Missionary Society. Kurt Emmerich, a German Jewish Christian, was the only survivor in his family but his wife came from a Nazi background. Some other refugees never arrived in Shaw! One Saturday afternoon it was announced that a trainload was expected from the continent and all the doctors and civic dignitaries waited in vain at the station for them. What happened to all the sandwiches prepared for them by the Coop nobody ever said. The mattresses put down in the Sunday schools were hurriedly removed before Sunday worship. The doctors decided there'd been a silly hoax and returned to their normal work.

Inside our home, life was very good. Jim was so easy to live with, so full of fun and in addition to his busy professional life he had so many interests and friends. With some truth people said he put more into his short forty years than many put into eighty. He had very clever hands and made beautiful models of ships and planes, a model railway and a doll's house with exquisite tiny furniture. We had dogs, cats, rabbits and tropical fish and Jim had always time for our own two girls as well as Cubs, Scouts and Rovers with whom he shared his interests.

In one sense World War II did not affect us and people like us very much; yet the changes that came with and after World War II affected us greatly. During the war the country needed women's work; in fact women were conscripted, mostly, I think, to work in munitions factories and agriculture. Their service was invaluable to the war effort. Consequently after the war married women were allowed to work – all the old-fashioned nonsense about them being preoccupied with romance and domestic life was forgotten. The changed attitude to women was later to affect me also.

In 1942 the Congregational Union launched the Reconstruction Fund with the purpose of building new churches after the end of hostilities. The Revd Howard Stanley came to advocate it in Shaw. I heard him at the ministers' fraternal and thought it was a splendid idea which had nothing to do with me. He rang up to say that a district commissioner was needed for Oldham and one man had turned down the job with a gift of £500 – would I do the job? I hadn't £500 with which to refuse but said, 'I have a little girl to look after.' Back came the comment, 'Isn't she a very good reason for rebuilding blitzed churches?' The point struck home, but I wasn't any good with money (except for spending it). Right – Jim would take on that part of the task if I would be advocate for the fund in the district. It proved a very successful joint effort.

Then Grandma Hendry, who couldn't come to terms with her dear husband's death, developed terminal cancer and came to spend her last months with us. Fortunately she wasn't in pain and was able to be up and about to the last days. Little Joyce gave her tremendous pleasure as they played games together. Of course there was no nearby play group or nursery school but fortunately the Smiths had two small children, a boy and girl, and their next-door neighbours had two little girls; with Joyce they made a very happy group of their own before they all went to the local Methodist school, where Mary Smith eventually taught.

During the war years, as petrol was not available for pleasure, I frequently took Joyce by bus to visit my aunt and uncle in Delph, four miles away in the West Riding of Yorkshire. Aunty Agnes had no children. She was my mother's only sister and still lived with her husband in the old family home. Perhaps because I had moved from one Methodist manse to another every three years until I was 25 I had a special affection for the old house at Delph, to which as a child I had often gone for holidays. It was built on a steep hillside – behind it was the meadow. Before my time my grandfather had started his woollen business in the big attic which the work people entered from the meadow. Later, he and his brother built Bailey Mill across the road from the house. His brother opted out, but until 1988 the mill belonged to the family. The building carefully planned by my grandfather has a warehouse opening on to the railway station platform. Consequently it has always been easy and economical to get raw wool and – having carded, spun and woven it – to despatch it as flannel, felt, baize, suitings and tartans all over the world. A descendant of my grandfather bearing his name, David Mallalieu, is the present manager for the new American owner. So the family business has gone the way of many more in the late 20th century.

When I was a child it was a thrill to go round the mill watching the various processes, standing by the gleaming noisy engine and playing around in the warehouse; but apart from the mill, Delph always was an important part in my life and I was glad to be able to take Joyce there to see Aunty. For one thing, to my prejudiced mind Delph seemed to belong to 'us'! There was the big house and farm where one uncle entertained an Indian prince and his doctor; another neighbouring house where the political branch of the family lived; in a third Aunty Mary presided with great dignity over her family of ten, and a fourth uncle had a house with a magnificent organ in the big hall. A number of married cousins lived round the village in more modest establishments.

Looking back, I remember a lot of the villagers too: there were the Murgatroyds who had a newsagent's shop and the Broadbents at the general stores; there was Handel Wood and the 'white sock' family, nicknamed from several of its daughters who came to the mill wearing clean white socks every day; we never did know their surname. Mary Ada Bilkey was a good friend of my mother and there was the Hudson family, vaguely related to us, whose Clarence composed popular hymntunes and whose Dora was always held up to me as a clever academic. These were all real individuals – characters to whom all our family related. They were not just employees or shopkeepers who served us, much less were they 'hands' who worked for faceless bosses, or cogs in a multinational machine. Sixty years on and miles away, I remember them clearly.

There were other well-to-do families with big houses in the valley and on the hillsides, but only on rare occasions did I visit them. At Shady Grove, when I took Joyce there, nothing much seemed to have changed since I was a child. Florrie Corns, the maid who had nursed me, was still there 30 years on to play with Joyce. One slight difference I couldn't fail to notice: where Aunty had made me stand in the kitchen to eat a biscuit while Florrie stood with the carpet sweeper at the ready, Joyce sat in a comfortable chair in the lounge and nobody seemed to notice the crumbs! When I rang up to arrange these war-time visits, Aunty always pleaded that they had only rations for three and therefore she couldn't provide anything special for tea. We were never short of food, so I always took a cake, or a packet of tea, or a pot of jam along with us.

In the week of D-day, 1945, news came that Uncle and Aunty had met with a bad car accident in Huddersfield; they both died although Aunty survived him for a very short time. Jim and I went over to Delph and found that Uncle had willed his considerable fortune to his sister's family but Aunty had left me the old house and its contents. Then the New Testament jumped into the 20th century! Florrie had to tell me that the attic was packed with goods 'laid up for many years'. There were new dustbins, pans, brushes, two to three years' supplies of soap, cleaning materials, and, under the floorboards, hoards of luxury tinned foods. On the shelves were jams and preserves to last a very long time. They had been so anxious about the future; suddenly all their precious stores were mine.

Florrie stayed several months until the house was sold, and we enjoyed many excellent meals there during that time. I was asked by other members of the family to conduct the funeral, and I thought how often Aunty had said she didn't know how she'd manage without Uncle; how often she'd told me they'd only rations for three and therefore couldn't prepare a special tea, and how dramatically the gospel story had come home to me. Since then I've visited Delph on many occasions, but now all my uncles and aunts have gone and I've no idea who lives in those old houses which once seemed so splendid. I know one was pulled down and a smaller one built on the site, and another was divided into four. Perhaps the American mill-owner lives in an old family house – I don't know; but back to 1945.

After the war ended churches began to invite me to take Sunday services, sometimes at a distance, and Jim gave me a little car which made such journeys possible. Because I had been ill during pregnancy, because war-time circumstances made life difficult and even more because Jim felt I ought not to risk a second pregnancy, we began to talk about adopting a second child. Joyce ran the risk as an only child of being thoroughly spoiled and she said she wanted a 'vacooee' to come and stay. Weren't thousands of war orphans needing homes? Wouldn't it be good to find a little girl to adopt? All we asked was that she should have a clean bill of health and be three or four years old. It sounded sensible and various agencies assured us there would be no problem; but nobody came up with a child for twelve months.

Then there was a scandalous case of a foster child being beaten up, and an enquiry was set up to investigate children in care. The local authority found that a little girl had come to Oldham with her mother from London after they had been bombed out. The father had been killed in the RAF. After some months the mother had disappeared leaving the child in hospital. As an abandoned child she was the responsibility of the public assistance department, as an evacuee she was in the care of the Ministry of Health. What should be done with her? She had been sent to a residential war-time nursery in Cumberland, so the authority had to find out how she was. A health visitor was sent north only to find that after two years the nursery had been closed, as all but three children had gone home. The remaining three had been put in a home for disturbed children.

The health visitor brought the three-year-old girl back to Oldham, and Jim and I met her in the public assistance office. If at that moment Jim's courage had failed, mine certainly would have done. She was such a pathetic little object – ill-nourished, dressed in shabby clothes from the Red Cross and with clogs on her feet. The officer suggested we took her home for the night and if we weren't satisfied we could bring her back; plenty of people in Oldham would be willing to give her a home. All her belongings were packed in a baby's gas-mask carton. Jim said, 'Come on, let's get her in the car' and I carried her, kicking and screaming, to the car, trying to reassure her that everthing would be alright. The contents of the carton were unusable, and almost immediately we took her and Joyce to the shoe shop. The clogs she was wearing had nails that had torn her toes and the heels were so worn down that her calf muscles had been stretched so that it took two years' therapy to correct her walking.

Quite quickly the wee soul realised that life had changed for the better; Joyce was extremely good with her and it wasn't long before Barbara was asking, 'Can I stay here? You won't send me away will you? Can I have my dinner here tomorrow?' The authorities said they wished she'd never come to us as Jim berated them for their gross neglect of the child who had been in their care, and we learned what damage can be done by tired overworked housemothers with too many children to look after. How naive we were in thinking we could take a child who had had such a bad start and by sharing our home with her all would be well. Of course it would have been far easier to adopt a six-wek old baby. One or two of our friends obviously thought we were idiotic, though Granny and most others accepted Barbara unreservedly. The problems didn't go away, but 40 years on I'm bound to say I would do what we did all over again, and I know that Jim never regretted Barbara's adoption. We made mistakes in dealing with her, but she herself always maintained that life would have been far worse if we had rejected her.

In addition to Jim's professional enthusiasm and love of the family, his great interest was the Scout movement. In Blantyre he had started a Scout company in the Anderson Church, and as Commissioner in Shaw he spent many evenings with Rover groups, giving talks and cine film shows, and with Cubs, playing with his splendid model railway. In the winter he gave them and the Scouts firework parties and in the summer took them to the local fair. Shaw Scouts for many years had the use of rather rough moorland on the edge of the town for camping. The farmer who owned it left the district and Jim bought 11 acres so that it could be kept for the use of Scouts. Some time later a man went to the surgery and said, 'Doctor, I owe you three years' rent for grazing sheep on your land.' Jim was amazed, especially when the man went on to say, 'Will you take payment in bacon?' for rationing was still in force. The site is still in use as the Anderson Scout Camp (in recognition of Jim's home church troop.)

Chapter 8

Second innings

In 1948 the Revd David Smith was called to Albion Congregational Church, Ashton-under-Lyne, a nonconformist cathedral of the North with a splendid history and challenge. He had served Shaw well during nine difficult years and everybody in the town regretted his departure. The deacons invited the moderator to discuss with them the church's future and made the suggestion that perhaps for an interim period I might act as caretaker-minister. He replied that it was a bad idea – if they wanted me back, why didn't they ask me to return as fulltime minister? The deacons felt I wouldn't be willing as I most certainly didn't 'need to work'. The moderator came to talk to Jim and me. Jim would be very happy for me to go back into the ministry at Shaw. He would provide more domestic help, I had my own car, the girls were at school all day, and I would not be chasing round the country to various churches on Sundays. And so it came about that the church re-called me, and we believed God had opened the way for me to serve again. Because of the unique circumstances, it was agreed that I should take a reduced stipend of £300 per year. The manse was let – it stood just five houses away from where we lived – and Jim laughingly declared it cost him money to have his wife working, but he didn't mind that.

I had been out of pastoral charge for 10 years and during those years a social revolution had taken place. One result of the war was the improvement in the economic situation. The terrible depression and poverty of the '30s had gone, although Shaw folk were not 'nouveau riche'. Things could never be the same after Hiroshima and the atom bomb, but the catastrophic disasters probably stimulated research and discovery in the medical profession. In the churches there was a desire for reconciliation which led to new links with Germans in the churches of the Rhineland Palatinate, but for the most part Shaw had not changed dramatically. There were no black faces in the community, for example, when I returned to work in 1948.

At the time of our marriage, I think ours was a unique professional partnership. In those days if anybody died, even if the family were not churchgoers, it was customary for the immediate circle of relatives and friends to attend three Sunday evening services following the funeral. Sometimes occasionally a permanent relationship was established.

One incident in which Jim asked for my help occurred one Sunday afternoon. Mrs B was terminally ill but was restless and Jim felt she had 'something on her mind' preventing her from dying. I went to see her and heard how for years she had carried the guilty secret that her daughter was the illegitimate child of a famous pianist. Having 'confessed', she soon died quietly and peacefully. Many years later my son-in-law, a Jungian analyst, complained about the harm 'the Church' has done to people in its teaching on sin, and the longer I live the more convinced I am that God is not obsessed about sex as churchmen have been and are.

Mrs S was a widow greatly venerated by Shaw Congregational Church; she had no home and lived in digs. She often made gifts to the church and on one occasion excelled her own generosity by presenting a beautiful blue carpet for the area round the communion table and blue seating for the choir stalls. I thanked her on behalf of the church. Then one evening I helped Jim with his accounts – this was prior to 1948 – and I found she owed him considerably more money than the cost of the carpet and paid the debt collector sixpence per week towards the debt. In no uncertain terms Jim told me who had given me and the church the new carpet.

Sometimes hospital staff were taken aback when I was visiting, to find out my profession. On one occasion I stopped to ask at the desk the whereabouts of a patient. One of the two men on duty greeted me, 'Yes love, and what can I do for you, love?' Whereupon his colleague intervened with, 'Shut up, you fool, she's a bloody parson!'

Was my recall to the ministry the happy result of our venture of faith in 1938? Jim was as confident as I was that we had been and were still guided by the Holy Spirit. And all went well for us... until 1950. For some months Jim had realised he had got leg trouble – intermittent claudication (a circulatory failure) hindered his walking. He couldn't keep up with the Scouts, and we could no longer enjoy dancing. He had inherited Buerger's Disease from his father, and in the summer of 1950 decided he must have an operation. Professor Boyd in Manchester was chairman of the World Council for Vascular Diseases and would himself operate at Manchester Infirmary. It would mean ten days in hospital; then I could drive us all for a Cornish holiday and Jim would be fit to drive back. A sympathectomy was a fairly routine operation.

Things went wrong. Jim had a massive thrombosis which led to the amputation of one leg, and Professor Boyd told me that his circulatory system was in such a bad condition I would never have freedom from anxiety. He might have a cerebral haemorrhage, a coronary thrombosis or a thrombosis in his other leg. Jim knew more accurately than I did how bleak the prospect was. He suffered excruciating pain, and many weeks went by before he was home. The church was most patient as I merely went through the routine motions of work. By Christmas Jim was able to get around on crutches and his colleagues shouldered the burdens of the practice. Dr Maitland, having survived the war as a locum in the Isle of Wight, had come back to Shaw to work as Jim's assistant and a local hospital lent a registrar to the practice. In January 1951 Jim decided he could do a little surgery work and greeted the patients cheerily with 'Anybody want to see a doctor – well here's half of one!'

February 8 1951 was a cold winter's day. About 10.30 am our family doctor, who had been called to our surgery, brought Jim home saying he must go to bed and he would call back later in the morning. Slowly Jim went upstairs; Ethel brought us both coffee, and within minutes I went down to the kitchen to say, 'The doctor is dead.' When our family doctor came back he was devastated.

Numbly I went through the routine of preparing for a funeral, and the girls had to be met when they came home from school. A representative deacon came to say the church would like to pay for the funeral, but I couldn't let them do that. There couldn't be a service in the church as it was closed for decoration, so the ceremony took place at Rochdale crematorium. Knowing that in the future I would have to conduct other funerals there, I asked for music which was not usually played there, and David Smith conducted the service. The girls insisted on going to school as usual but came home early to see the Scots relatives. When the church asked for a student supply for the Sunday services the college principal came personally, and the following week, in the Sunday school building packed to capacity, the moderator conducted a service of thanksgiving.

We were all magnificently supported by the church and by Jim's medical and scouting colleagues, but at the time I hardly knew how arrangements were made and work was done. Ethel, Granny and the gardener didn't trouble me with any domestic chores – I heard Joyce comment to Barbara how normal everything was. It was three weeks later that I suddenly realised Jim's Scout Commissioner's hat was still in the hall and immediately asked the gardener to burn it. Numbness was passing, and painful tasks had to be done. Obviously the big Rover car, the gardener, the daily help, the orchids and the tropical fish, the stamp collection and all the Scouting gear must go. Our handsome income had stopped and I was lucky that the mortgage had been paid off and it was possible for me to stay in the house and have Ethel. The deacons immediately decided that I must have £400 per year instead of £300.

I couldn't see how life would develop. I was responsible for two little girls and I owed a debt of gratitude to the church which was so loyal and generous to me. I just wanted to stay where people knew Jim and where we had been so happy. If anyone had forecast that I would have a Scout grandson, I wouldn't have believed them. Just a fortnight after her father's death, Joyce sat the 11-plus examination of the Lancashire authority. Although she and Barbara were already at Oldham Hulme Grammar School for girls in the preparatory department, as they had been four years in a state junior school Joyce was eligible to sit, and did so well that the county agreed to pay her fees at Hulme. The school had a splendid head who was exceptionally understanding about our situation, and particularly about Barbara.

Jim's death brought back all her feelings of insecurity; she said to me, 'God is very cruel – he's taken a mother and two Daddys from me and I'm only nine... If you die, I'll kill myself.' Her school work was poor and on one occasion when I was very angry about a bad report she flashed back, 'Mummy, I'm top of the failures!' Fortunately Barbara never lacked a self-defence mechanism! Optimistic teachers assured me she would eventually make the grade, and she did, by getting her SRN, followed by midwifery and other special nursing qualifications.

One of Jim's consultant friends often came to see how we were getting on, and when Joyce was about 16 asked her what she wanted to do. She would have to go for science, she said, possibly pharmacy. Grandpa Hendry had been a chemist. 'Would you go in for research?' the doctor asked and got the answer, 'I want to work with people.' 'Joyce,' was his reply, 'as a scientist you know where you can best work with people.' The seed took root and shortly after that conversation Joyce announced, 'I'm going to be a doctor.' When she went to Edinburgh for an interview, a member of the faculty said to her, 'I see your father was a doctor and your mother is a minister of religion – why do you want to be a doctor?' She replied, 'Because I believe God is calling me to continue my father's work.' Seven years had gone by since that disastrous day in February 1951.

Chapter 9

In need of healing

On the day of Jim's funeral, Granny had caught me making up my face, with a lipstick in my hand. 'If you feel lousy,' I told her, 'there's no point in looking lousy.' I'd been taught not to be a cry-baby. Our good doctor said I was living on my pride and he felt that he, as Jim's GP, had nothing to be proud of. The new locum who came to live with us for a while insisted on conducting endless post mortems in my evenings till I could bear them no longer.

I'd never dealt with insurance, quarterly bills, car repairs and a dozen other chores which I loathed. I found there were 'smart alecs' around who were anxious to take Jim's orchids off my hands at a ridiculously low price; and there was the stupid comment of the man who said, 'I should think you'll give up preaching now' and an equally stupid comment from a woman: 'If you'd known this was going to happen, you needn't have had Barbara.' I was so sorry for myself! The quality of my routine ministry must have been very poor, but the church didn't complain.

Often when I drove up the hill at teatime, a ten-year-old curly-headed boy across the road would shout, 'Hi, Mrs Hendry!' He could never know that he helped me to go in and face the girls. Granny, who had little to say and no advice to offer, proved invaluable as the listener who put up with my moaning and never repeated my outbursts to anyone. At night when I cried 'Why? Why?' the heavens seemed as brass – and yet somehow, as my days so was my strength. Life had to go on. The girls were my responsibility; they needed me. Sometimes since, bereaved people have asked which is worse – to lose your partner so early, or after the family has grown up and left home so that you are alone with no-one dependent on you. My answer is that the burden of responsibility – the fact that I was needed – helped to keep me sane, until gradually I acquired the ability to cope single-handed, and some lessons learned the hard way began to prove useful when I met other people in trouble. At 35 years' distance, I can now say that if Jim had not died, in all probability I would never have had the exciting opportunities of a developing ministry, but the price paid in the '50s for my future was very high.

Looking after the congregation at Shaw was sufficiently demanding to keep me occupied, and at the same time left me some spare hours for other work. I became a member of the Divisional Education Authority, Chairman of Governors at Chadderton Grammar School for Girls, a member of the Lancashire Education Committee representing the Free Churches, a Governor of Silcoates School representing the Lancashire Congregational Union, and Governor and sometime Chairman of the Education Committee of my own old college in Manchester. These appointments widened my experience beyond the small town of Shaw, and the local church kindly took the view that these interests enhanced my ministry in the church. Maybe they did a bit, but I knew that if I were a better minister than before, it was because I had myself suffered. Like Ezekiel, I could sit where my people sat, and until one does get alongside people it is very difficult to serve them.

One day as I was visiting a hospital patient on behalf of a colleague, a nurse came and asked if I would go and speak to Mrs Mills.

'Who is she? I don't know her.'

'She's the blind woman in the bed opposite and she's recognised your voice...'

Mrs Mills told me she had that day lost her faith in God. She had heard a doctor tell Sister she would never recover her fingers' sensitivity and be able to read Braille or work again at the workshop for the blind. She was 36. When her husband had dropped dead after six months' happy marriage she'd become totally blind, but had made valiant efforts and carried on earning her living; but God had now blinded her twice and her faith was finished. She said 'I know you've lost your husband. I thought you might understand!' The comment has been made many times since that day and usually by people in far more tragic circumstances than mine.

During recent years the church in all the denominations has turned its attention to the ministry of healing. Thirty years ago I saw that ministry from a different angle. There were four medical practices in Shaw – two staffed by four doctors and two by two doctors. I knew all six doctors, as well as a number of consultants in Oldham and nursing staff at several hospitals, and they all knew me. Because of the high regard they'd had for Jim, they were all eager to support me and the girls. I broke my ankle, and the top orthopaedic surgeon and chief anaesthetist in Oldham dealt with it. Help was immediate in the middle of the night when Barbara developed appendicitis; and much later when Joyce was a medical student she was invited to sit in with a consultant physician at his clinic and stand at a surgeon's side in the operating theatre.

On one occasion a deacon of my church asked if I would go and see his wife, S, who was depressed and unable to cope with their children, a four-year-old girl and a baby five months old. After talking with her, I suggested that she saw her doctor but she refused. The last time she'd been to the surgery he had been cross; however she agreed that I should ring him up. His answer to me was, 'Let's go together – when will be convenient to you?' He recommended her to wean the baby and to some extent restored her confidence. The same week I was having supper with a distinguished gynaecologist and told him how valuable I thought my co-operation with the local GPs was. Somewhat cynically he said we weren't likely to achieve much. I was furious with him. I was quite sure S was beginning to improve.

A few nights later, after a teachers' meeting, her husband rushed to tell me that he had come home to find the door open, the children in bed asleep, dinner for the next day prepared and a good fire built up for the night, but his wife had vanished. He had got his parents to stay with the children and then came for me. Would I send for the police, would I tell the doctor? Quickly the police arrived and the doctor asked me to phone back as soon as there was any news. The police suggested I should take the husband in my car to every house where he thought she might have gone. Rain was pouring in torrents and he was sure the exercise would be useless; it was. So he, his parents and I sat and waited in his home. About 11.30 pm there was a knock at the door. The police sergeant asked to speak to me – would I please tell the family she had thrown herself under a bus and was dead at Oldham Infirmary. They would wait and take her husband there in a police car. When he got back he insisted on feeding the baby and then asked if I would pray with him and his parents before going home.

It was 2 am, and going home I saw a downstairs light at the doctor's. I rang the bell and told the doctor, 'She's thrown herself under a bus'. Quite sharply he answered, 'Who says so?' Then he insisted I go to the police station and tell them the incident ought to be treated as an accident. They were sympathetic (Jim had been police surgeon) but Shaw worked under the Lancashire County authority and she was dead in Oldham, which was a different authority. They advised me to go next morning with her husband to Oldham. There the police asked me, 'Who the hell are you?' but they listened to me. So there were no insinuating headlines in the local paper, no suggestions that a young wife had been neglected by a husband heavily involved in church work, no statement that the mother of two little girls had committed suicide. At the inquest my gynaecologist friend paid for a solicitor, whose services weren't needed when a verdict of accidental death was returned.

At the time the husband, in a state of shock, didn't think it mattered whether his wife was dubbed a suicide or not, but later he and all the family appreciated the doctor's foresight. The family was poor and his parents had always been so, but without a word his mother gave up her work in the mill to look after the children, unpaid. Some years later the bereaved husband made a second happy marriage and to this day all the family continue to serve the same church in Shaw. I have told this story at length because I learned so much about healing through that experience and realised how the Church could support and care in a long-term situation working alongside doctors and social workers.

The story of Kitty illustrates the harshness of the authority towards the most vulnerable members of society. Kitty had come to Lancashire from Scotland during the first World War. She had lived with a local publican for some 20 years and on his retirement they had moved into a tiny cottage. He became ill and senile and was permanently in the old general hospital. Because of his permanence there, the authority claimed all his financial assets, so Kitty had no source of income. One very cold winter's day I found her clad only in vest and skirt and clogs with no fire in the house. She'd had no food for three days. I went to the Public Assistance Office where the official reminded me that she had been 'living in sin for 20 years'. She was not the man's wife and therefore was no concern of that office. Infuriated, I retorted that we didn't allow dogs to starve and unless he did something for Kitty I would go straight to the local newspaper office and hand them the story. I also pointed out that it would be more expensive to take her into care than to give her a weekly allowance for food and fuel. Commonsense won that day and Kitty was looked after by the authority and by the church for the rest of her life. Injustice to the poor has always roused my anger and when I was in Shaw it was usually possible to do something about it.

Another case of cruel injustice of a very different kind also involved me in a prolonged dispute with authority. Our friend the gynaecologist who had been in charge of the local general hospital was dismissed from his post because of a row about an abortion. He had angered some Roman Catholic members of staff who had reported his conduct, with the result that when his contract ran out he was left without a new one. Hundreds of grateful patients and many colleagues were extremely upset and the Free Church Federal Council asked me to help with a petition to the Government for his reinstatement. Altogether the campaign took something like seven years and went eventually to the House of Lords, where the wrong was righted and the doctor was reinstated. It was a rare occasion on which an individual prevailed over the Ministry of Health; but the anguish of those years had been very hard to bear and all too soon afterwards the doctor dropped dead at a meeting. How often it must have happened that faceless authorities have destroyed people – and continue to do so. Injustice still makes me angry, but I am not in a position to fight as I once did.

As the '50s ran their course my girls were growing apace and my own professional life was opening out in ways never anticipated. I was lucky enough to go to the International Congregational Council at St Andrews in 1954 and to Hartford, Connecticut in 1958 as President of the Federation of Congregational Women; then to Rotterdam in 1962 where Joyce and Barbara were able to be with me to celebrate Barbara's 21st birthday. But questions were looming on the horizon. The girls were preparing to leave home in pursuit of their own careers. How long could I stay in Shaw? Till I retired at 60? At 65? What opportunities could there be for me elsewhere? Older male ministers were finding it difficult to move; churches wanted younger leaders full of vigour and new ideas. At 59 it looked as if my working life was nearly over. How wrong can one be?

About this time I was Chairman of Governors at Chadderton Grammar School for Girls where my friend Dorothy Myatt, a keen Methodist, was headmistress. The head of the Religious Education Department, a Methodist minister, died unexpectedly and Dorothy suggested that I should apply for his post. It was an attractive idea. I knew the school well and was on good terms with many members of the staff. The salary with graduate allowances etc was nearly four times what I was earning, and I was living in my own house which was expensive to maintain. I told Dorothy I believed God had called me to be a minister. She retorted, couldn't God vary that call in a useful ministry to girls and staff in her school? A ministerial colleague argued that if I deserted pastoral charge I was letting the side down – just as certain critics had said when I married. In the end, thinking few working years were left, I turned the idea of teaching down; but the question stayed – What ought I to do? One day in 1965, journeying with the moderator to a Governors' Meeting at Silcoates School, the conversation turned to the problems of older ministers and I voiced the opinion that it would be very difficult for me to get another call. Within weeks three churches made approaches to me, one in Cheshire and two in Lancashire. I chose Clitheroe. The other two churches also called women ministers.

Chapter 10

The river flows, the rock stands

Clitheroe is 29 miles from Shaw, but it is a world away. An old proverb has it that Clitheroe is noted for Law, Lime and Latin. Its history of 1,000 years is commemorated in the old quarries so noted for fossils, in its castle and parish church and in the beautiful Ribble Valley and Pendle Hill. In contrast to the stern, often harsh life of Shaw, life in Clitheroe is not poverty-stricken. It has lingering feudal traditions, a lot of courtesy and gracious living. It is a flourishing town with an excellent sense of community and well-established ecumenical relationships. With my Aberdeen terrier Mac, I pulled up the roots in Shaw and drove into this new situation in December 1965. A few weeks later Granny joined me. Life would be easier in Clitheroe! Having left the Manchester District of the Lancashire Congregational Union I had lost my place on many committees although I would still go to Preston as Free Church representative on the County Education Committee and to Silcoates School.

Driving on pastoral visits through the quiet leafy lanes or for pleasure over the fells, I couldn't stop thinking how fortunate I was; and I lived in a manse with a salary twice as big as I'd had in Shaw. My family were pleased; at last Mum was having an easier life – she had dropped many responsibilities to concentrate on the pastoral care of a church that had a goodly number of capable lay people and of the tiny village church at Barrow near Whalley with just 32 members: and once again I hadn't the least idea of the unfolding future.

In April 1966 my elder daughter Joyce, now a qualified GP like her father, was married in my church to John Carlisle, a Jungian analyst who had also trained in Edinburgh. After a mild winter that was the only day when Clitheroe had snow! – but it was a splendid occasion in which the church joined. Both Joyce and Barbara returned to Scotland after the wedding but Clitheroe was such a friendly place I didn't feel lonely, although there were days when I grieved that I now lived among people who had not known Jim Hendry.

One of the gains of life in Clitheroe was that I was welcomed into a wide circle of friends not all connected with my church. Dr Royle's wife Monica had been at school with me; the headmaster of the Royal Grammar School for boys and his wife Molly were Anglicans. She and I found much in common, as she was a social worker. The headmistress of the Girls' Grammar School, an Anglican, became a personal friend, as did Nell whose husband belonged to the Congregational Church. He was a very well-known geologist as well as a local textile manufacturer. My own church secretary and his wife Kate with their big family were a great support in a hundred ways. The musical society in Blackburn opened up further interest for me, and altogether life was full and happy.

In the church there were very few children at first: however with the formation of uniformed boys' organisations, Cubs and Scouts, jointly with the Methodists, and with Brownies and Guides closely connected with nearby Waddow Hall, an international training centre for Guiders, numbers increased considerably. Like my father before me, I had always believed strongly in the importance of work with children and young people in the Church. As a girl I had been a Guide and later a lieutenant in the Guide movement. I have already mentioned the great numbers of boys and girls in Scout and Guide Companies in Shaw but until I went to Clitheroe I'd very little experience of youth work outside these organisations. For a while I'd run a girl's club in Shaw which was little more than an opportunity for chat, with occasional outings, playing netball and hiking.

In Clitheroe the situation with children and young people was quite different. There was a distinct church group of splendid youngsters and teenagers - the children of church families who had many privileges. There were hundreds more young people in the town who did not belong to any church or any uniformed organisation. The town itself had admirable facilities geared to grown-up interests and to highly specialised pursuits like ornithology and geology, but apart from a somewhat rundown coffee shop there was little for teenagers. The town had the second highest rate of juvenile delinquency in Lancashire, according to the police.

Several of the churches had 'closed' youth clubs which went out of existence from time to time. The Congregational church housed an open club – some 300 strong – to which none of the church youth group went. If a pane of glass got broken, if anything was missing, if a meeting was disturbed by noise, if rooms were found untidy, it was 'that youth club's' fault – until Mick became the leader! He was not a churchgoer but excellently trained and quite wonderful in the way he could handle young people. There was no-one in the church who could have done what he did, and more than once social workers said the youth club was the only lifeline they had with some teenagers. Relations with the church improved and the youth club not only accepted responsibility for damage but generously contributed to church funds; and during my stay in Clitheroe it was the only club that was never seriously vandalised and never closed down. The police were cooperative and appreciative of the community service rendered. I learned not to be frightened by big lads with masses of fuzzy black hair, some of whom called me the Vicaress. The police were always at hand when rumour had it that Hell's Angels proposed an invasion of the town. In return Mick kept them informed about the drug scene.

During the late '60s and '70s Clitheroe had quite a large number of Pakistani immigrants, mostly Moslems, who worked at the ICI and Ribble Cement works. The churches made efforts to integrate them, as well as a number of Polish and Italian people in the town. Eventually an international club was formed and we got to know quite a number of families personally, but it proved extremely difficult to involve the Pakistani women in community affairs. For the most part they stayed at home and couldn't be persuaded to join in outings to the countryside or Lancaster or Skipton or even to parties with oriental food – and their menfolk gave them no encouragment to do so. It was easier with the children who, of course, went to local schools and spoke English fluently. On at least one occasion some of the Moslems joined with us in an evening service of worship. Blackburn, the nearest big town 12 miles away, had a large Hindu community who apparently were happily settled there and certainly had good relations with one of our ministers and his church.

Clitheroe Congregational Church belonged to the Blackburn District of the Lancashire Congregational Union and in the area there was only one Presbyterian church. Alan Gaunt had been my predecessor in Clitheroe; Graham Cook and Tony Burnham, later to move to national office, were ministerial colleagues in the district, but I held no District office and thought committee days were done. Looming on the horizon was the new United Reformed Church, and I found myself called to London more or less monthly to share in structuring the new Church. This meant driving 20 miles to Preston to catch the 7 am train and coming back home between 9 and 10 pm. Years earlier I had vowed never to go to London and back in a day – but the train service from Preston was usually very good and the driving was easy. By 1968 Joyce and John had moved south and their son Bruce was born in Croydon in July that year, so visits to London were very happy occasions when I could stay with the family overnight; but I was more and more content to stay north in Clitheroe.

The church to which I was called, built of white limestone that glistened in the sunshine, stands at the gate of the castle in the centre of the town. The castle itself is one of the oldest stone buildings in Lancashire and the smallest Norman keep in England. The splendid town motto is, 'The river flows, the rock stands'. Both the church and the castle are built on rock and all the life of the town flows by their doors.

The three Ls for which Clitheroe is noted refer to the fact that the castle for centuries was the administrative centre of the extensive Honour of Clitheroe granted to Roger de Poitou in the 11th century. Lime was burnt at Clitheroe for centuries and was the town's oldest manufacturing industry. The reference to Latin alludes to the royal Grammar School, founded by charter of King Philip II of Spain and Queen Mary in 1554, 'for the instruction, education and learning of boys and young men in the art of grammar'. In the Civil War, in 1648, Oliver Cromwell passed through Clitheroe on his way to Preston and spent the night at Stonyhurst where, it is told, 'fearful of assassination he slept on the refectory table, his sword at his side'.

With the Restoration of the monarchy and in 1662 the passing of the Act of Uniformity, some 2,000 of the Puritan clergy resigned their benefices rather than conform to the Act. One of them was the Revd Thomas Jollie, who took refuge at Wymondhouses on the slopes of Pendle Hill and whose ministry is commemorated in Barrow URC, which was known as the Jollie Memorial Congregational Church. Those were hard times for dissenters and no doubt the area was difficult for religious pioneers, yet there were several independent churches in the neighbourhood for people who would walk 20 miles or more to worship God in the ways they thought right. The seclusion of places like Horton in Paradise, Newton-in-Bowland and Wymondhouses gave some protection from the persecution and injustices which were endured by the forefathers of Congregationalism in North-east Lancashire.

In the 17th century George Fox, the founder of the Quaker movement, recorded a visit to the area: 'As we travelled we came near a very great hill called Pendle Hill and I was moved of the Lord to go up to the top of it, which I did with difficulty, it was so very steep and high. When I was come to the top I saw the sea bordering upon Lancashire, and there on the top I was moved to sound the day of the Lord, and the Lord let me see in what places He had a great people to be gathered.' I never climbed Pendle on foot. I lived within its shadow and often on a clear day I drove up to the Nick of Pendle and looked out to Blackpool and thought about Fox's words. A great sense of history lingered in Clitheroe and I loved it and its people.

Officially Congregationalism began in Clitheroe in 1817, just after the Napoleonic War, when the Revd Joseph Wadsworth became the first minister of the little church built in 1815 at the cost of £700. It was not until the 1860s that the present church was erected, at the cost of £3,850 plus £850 for the site. In 1967 we celebrated the church's triple jubilee. A booklet was produced whose writer commented, 'the histories of town and church reveal an ever moving pattern of events, an unceasing flow of changing circumstances, people and politics: as inevitable and irreversible as the flowing river on whose banks the town is set. It is impossible not to recognise that those who have gone before and taken part in changing events have always had a vision – sometimes splendid and clear, sometimes faint and blurred – of a rock immovable and steadfast. The work of their faith stands. That the river flows and the rock stands must also be the message of the future. We can expect nothing but changes and we can expect that they will come with increasing rapidity, but our faith is also that the purpose of God will as surely stand. Many of the changes which we are facing will tend to disrupt further, and maybe disintegrate a local society which is already less coherent and tight knit than in the days when this church was first formed. In so far as the mission of the church is directed towards the needs of people in society, the church must change to meet these new needs despite its inclination to cling to the traditions of the past. No longer will a church whose organisation is based on the needs of a static semi-rural population be adequate.'

The town's motto caught my own imagination. In many ways my own experience was like a flowing river. I had moved on from the bleak hills of Shaw to the fertile valley with its softer climate and gentler ways, but the rock of faith on which my life was built stood firm. I had been made to repeat, 'as I was with Moses so I will be with thee' and I had proved the words true. It was good to share in the pleasant stable life of Clitheroe church and the historic town that was so friendly to an incomer.

Much has been written about the Swinging Sixties - but that decade in Clitheroe was not marked by dramatic social changes. Church work continued steadily. The Council of Churches organised excellent Lent courses and its members worked well together to study the so-called Third World and raise considerable sums of money for Christian Aid and Cafod. In our church we were particularly fortunate. The church secretary and his wife opened their home every week to the church youth group who undertook some really serious study of world affairs. One of the girls in the church, having graduated in Edinburgh, became a candidate for the ministry – a highly successful student at the Manchester College. For some obscure reason I became increasingly involved in the Church's ministerial training in Manchester and London where, to my bewilderment, I was elected as committee chairman, a position usually occupied by a senior academic. I never did justice to the task but was tremendously thrilled to have it.

In 1970 my grand-daughter Sheena was born in Croydon and we were all delighted, but afterwards Joyce became desperately ill with a thrombosis in a deep pelvic vein. The chances of survival were slim. Clitheroe freed me to go and look after Bruce, then two years old. For some days the tension and anxiety were almost unbearable and of course the patient herself knew just how bleak the prospect was. Mercifully she recovered; the support from many church friends was unforgettable, and very close ties were made between me and Bruce. During that crisis I had plenty of time to think about faith and doubt, about praying for miracles and about tragedies other people had to endure. We were all supremely grateful Joyce's life was saved and as the years have gone by that gratitude has deepened as she has devoted herself and her considerable skills to bringing health and happiness to so many people. At Christmas 1970 Sheena was baptised in the Clitheroe Church as Bruce had been in 1968.

In 1972 the family invited me to join them on holiday at St Mary's in the Isles of Scilly. It was a delightful prospect, but the dates overlapped with a church leaders' conference in Birmingham and the General Secretary of the Congregational Church had asked me to go. I wrote and asked him if I might be excused and he said No! Driving down the M6 it was tempting to bypass Birmingham and go on to Penzance. I didn't want to go to Birmingham, and in any case what contribution could I offer that couldn't have been bettered by somebody else? Never was I more reluctant to do anything than I was to go to Birmingham in September '72.

Out of 500 representatives from all the major denominations in Britain there were only 29 women there. On arrival I met a Presbyterian who admitted to being as unwilling as I was. Then things began to change, and whatever any other members of that assembly gained from it, I found it exciting and stimulating. I well remember the future Bishop of Durham's word, 'There is more to God than Jesus'; but the lecture by Ian Ramsey, then Bishop of Durham, on the Crisis of Faith made an indelible impression. It was at Birmingham that the Archbishop of Canterbury (Dr Coggan) asked me how long I'd been ordained. Forty years! He said it was time the Church of England woke up. In a masterly summing-up of the experience, Methodist Kenneth Greet spoke of the need for a new style in leadership – a leadership that would listen and say 'come', rather than 'go'. September 1972 convinced me that 'consensus' is right and 'confrontation' wrong, and that interdependence must be recognised in the kind of world we have.

At Birmingham I met Pauline Webb, perhaps the best-known woman leader in the Methodist Church as I write, who also gives distinguished service to the World Council of Churches and broadcasting. Her father had been the Methodist minister in Shaw when I was a mum pushing a pram. Pauline went to the grammar school of which I was a governor. It was a humbling moment when she told me how seeing me about Shaw and knowing I was an ordained minister had set her thinking about her own future. Unlike me, she did not leave the Methodist Church which would not ordain her, but I suspect she couldn't possibly have made a greater contribution to the World Church if she had been ordained. In 1987 I met her again and heard her speak in Croydon and again she referred to the years in Shaw and reminded me of the wonderful help she'd received from Jim, who had been her doctor. One of the joys of old age is to discover the value and influence of seeming small incidents long lost to memory.

October 1972 saw the inauguration of the United Reformed

Church and following so quickly on the Birmingham Conference I felt I had been caught up in tremendous events. Happily, I was honoured to have a place in Westminster Abbey at the inaugural service and my daughter Joyce was able to share the day with me. For months I had been coming regularly to London to work on structuring the new Church's committees. It was great to share in that work – it was more splendid to be present on October 5 to celebrate the first union of two denominations in this country since the Reformation. Never had I imagined the day when I and my daughter would be able to say 'we were there'. What a climax to my long years as a 'general practitioner in the ministry', and I had still a job to do in Clitheroe before retiring. Life was very good indeed, even though I was over the hill. I've always guessed wrong about the future.

When the minister at Newton-in-Bowland, Horton in Paradise and Martin Top had to leave because Horton and Martin Top did not join the URC and Newton alone wasn't a full-time job, the members there opted to join in the group with Clitheroe and Barrow. Newton and Barrow had almost identical numbers of adults – around 32 – and they were both the only places of worship in the two villages; yet no two churches could be more unlike each other. Barrow had a day school attached; there were about 30 pupils and they were so privileged in comparison with most junior schools in the care of the Lancashire county. They had adequate staffing and every piece of modern equipment asked for; Pendle Hill was the background to their full-size cricket field, their tarmacadamed play area and pavilion. It was so different from some of the schools I'd known in the Shaw area which hardly boasted flagged playgrounds and were always short of teachers and equipment.

Newton is a conservation area nestling in the fells seven miles from Clitheroe. To drive there from Clitheroe always reminded me of the Scottish highlands. There were about 48 houses in the village – a general store and butcher's and the Parkers Arms (recently I think the shops, but not the pub, have closed). No new houses can be built in the village. A barn or two has been levelled and rebuilt as a home but because of the conservation order young people are compelled to leave and find new homes for themselves in Clitheroe or elsewhere.

Newton in the '70s had 100 per cent membership of village children in the church – they numbered fourteen, five of whom were one family and four from another. Church meeting was held once a year and usually leaders were re-elected en bloc; but Newton had a wider ministry. Because of its lovely situation, summer coachloads of trippers came from Leeds and elsewhere to enjoy teas provided and services shared at Newton; and the links with Clitheroe were very good, so that the choir and other members from Clitheroe enjoyed going to swell the congregation on special occasions. It was easy to operate the union of the three churches. Clitheroe had a morning service with an evening service once a month, Newton had an afternoon service and Barrow had morning and evening services. My daughters pointed out they thought I'd gone to Clitheroe to do less work!

The Blackburn District felt it right to celebrate the inauguration of the United Reformed Church in Blackburn, and so good were ecumenical relations that a magnificent service with communion took place in Blackburn Cathedral – with no restrictions. Dr John Marsh, theologian and former college principal, preached and was surprised by the freedom given to us by the Cathedral authorities.

The Clitheroe church had a structural problem. It had two entrance doors on to the main street so that it was impossible for the minister to shake hands with everybody as they went in or out. The secretary fortunately was a distinguished architect and proposed that the back pews be taken out and a glass screen dropped from the back gallery, so creating a common room for meeting people before and after worship. The scheme proved highly successful: from the common room one could look straight into the sanctuary, and the room itself proved a favourite meeting-place for coffee on Sundays and not infrequently during the week. That room in many ways is a bridge between the church and the town for which hundreds of people have been grateful.

In 1974 I was invited to represent the United Reformed Church at the Assembly of the Church of Scotland in Edinburgh, along with the Revds Arthur Macarthur and Howard Williams and Sir Harold Banwell. Scotland to me meant Jim and his family, some of whom still lived in Edinburgh. That year David Steel's father was the Moderator of Assembly and the Liberal leader's brother had married one of Joyce's university friends, so Joyce had met Mrs Steel. She invited me and a few others for tea during the Assembly. There was also the pleasure of a garden party at Holyrood House.

Not all the sessions of the Assembly were inspiring and there was one long dreary debate on the mutual eligibility of former Congregational ministers and ministers of the Church of Scotland. In the end commonsense prevailed and Arthur Macarthur murmured, 'Now Kathleen you can conduct the Communion Service in St Giles Cathedral!' Nearly 30 years previously I had conducted the Communion Service at the Anderson Church, Blantyre, where my father-in-law was an elder. Somehow I've always managed to break the rules!

We four United Reformed Church representatives together with Mrs Macarthur and Lady Banwell stayed in the same hotel, and as I came last one morning to the breakfast table the Revd Howard Williams stood up; embarrassed I asked him please to sit down. He said he always stood up for a lady, whereupon the Revd Arthur Macarthur exclaimed, 'But Kathleen isn't a lady. She's one of our ministers.' I liked that.

In Clitheroe I hadn't such a close association with the medical profession as I'd enjoyed in Shaw and Oldham because the doctors in Clitheroe had never known Jim, but on several occasions I was able to work with them. Naturally all efforts didn't result in success stories, but cooperation with the medical profession usually proved very helpful.

One of the loveliest old ladies in Clitheroe had lost her husband before I knew her. She had also lost a brilliant son in World War II. She lived with her second bachelor son who was a schizophrenic. Fortunately they had plenty of money and although her sight was failing the old lady knew every inch of the house. Usually she could cope with her son. One day as I visited she was upstairs changing her dress and the son began to cry to me that the following Tuesday, his birthday, the Martians were coming, and after killing his mother he was going to kill himself. When his mother came down she just said, 'Now B, let's have a bit less science fiction'. As I drove off I thought – what can I do? I'll invite them for tea on Tuesday. Later, phoning the family, I shared the incident with my son-in-law John, who said, 'You must do no such thing. If you want to help, phone his doctor and tell him how he is.' The doctor concerned was also my doctor and had the reputation of being extremely brusque and very intolerant of interference from parsons. At first I said, 'He'll bite my head off' – but then, what if he does? So I phoned him and he promptly exploded: 'What d'you expect me to do? I'm concerned about his mother.' I retorted 'So am I.' Gradually he calmed down and described how B wouldn't accept medication as he thought he was being poisoned. John told me the treatment being prescribed was the best available. The very next day the doctor paid B a visit. He proved to be a good friend and a good doctor to me.

Time went by; then the police were informed that B had sexually abused a number of boys. I went to court and heard that B was to be sent to Risley for psychiatric appraisal. Because of his mother's frailty I asked the police if I could go to Risley to see him. The sergeant at first said, 'No way must you go to Risley'. I pleaded, and on the advice of his senior officer I was allowed to go. That was a day of surprises! I really didn't know what kind of people got into trouble with the law, so it was a bit of a shock to find that my Triumph Herald car was the cheapest in the visitors' car park! The reception officer was amused that I was a parson, and commented on my hat. Guarded by a police officer and an Alsatian dog, I was taken to a small room with a table and two chairs to meet B. The chaplain was called in to listen to the conversation. I told B his mother sent her love. He burst into tears but when I offered a tissue the police officer said, 'No – he must wipe his nose on his shirt cuff'. I had taken the church newsletter. I could not give it to B until the police had read it. When we came out, the chaplain said, 'You mentioned his mother – he must be over 65'. 'No', I said, 'he's 44. That's what being here has done to him in three weeks – on remand for medical assessment!' Eventually B was put on three years' probation, the first to be spent in a very good private nursing home. The last I heard about him was that his mother having died, he was in a permanent home for the elderly.

This incident in Clitheroe wasn't the first occasion when I have been very disturbed about the methods of the penal system. Back in Shaw when I was out of pastoral charge I was invited to join with the local ministers in an evangelical campaign in the town. One night I went to the notorious Pineapple Inn and began chatting with a few people at the bar. Very soon a middle-aged woman was in tears and told me she was waiting to go to court on a charge of having done an illegal abortion for £3; the girl had died. To my horror she went on to say the girl had been one of Jim's patients – it was my husband who had reported the case. The woman was sentenced to three years in Strangeways prison in Manchester, so I went there to try to see her. No way could I be admitted – there was a prison chaplain; if I chose to write to her it would mean she could not have a letter from her family, as she was only allowed one letter a month.

The incident in Clitheroe happened 20 years later, and now that another 20 years have gone by, the way our society deals with offenders still seems to me uncivilised and unhelpful. I sometimes wish I had tried to do something about penal reform. I did try to help the woman's family in Shaw but I wasn't popular with them because of Jim's part in the case. Thank goodness properly conducted abortions are no longer illegal, but tremendous developments in genetic science have produced new ethical problems. I regret that in the new emphasis on the Church's ministry of healing, I don't see church groups tackling such questions or conferring with the medical profession about them. It seems to me that the churches still often work independently of the medical profession in their care for people. It was a Jewish doctor who asked me for advice about visiting bereaved families and I know only one minister who cooperates closely with local doctors about such matters.

Chapter 11

Going south

In 1974 Barbara, her husband Jimmy and their son Jeremy were living in South Wales where Jimmy was working with the British Oxygen Company. Joyce and her family were just moving to Purley, and she became concerned because they were all a long way from me and I was getting old. As she was in general practice she said she couldn't dash north if I suddenly had 'flu or some other illness – so wouldn't it be a good idea if I moved south and settled in another community before I was too old to make new friends? I saw the point – and mentioned to the moderator the fact that in certain circumstances I could be persuaded to go south, although I was quite sure I couldn't be happier anywhere than I was in Clitheroe. I had letters from two churches which didn't interest me at all, then one day at Silcoates School the moderator suggested another London church. I replied that I'd better consider it or else he would think me extremely choosy; but he went on, 'There's an assistant's post coming up in Purley. You wouldn't look at an assistant's job, would you?' Promptly I answered, 'I would in Purley - that's where my daughter Joyce and her family live!' The very next day the Revd Cyril Franks, Purley's minister, 'phoned and I was invited down to Purley. It seemed nothing less than providential. There was actually a second manse at Purley – who else at 68 could be so lucky? Never had I thought life could begin again at my age, and never had I imagined a ministry outside Lancashire.

In recent years much has been said and written about the north-south divide in Britain. I doubt whether my father ever visited the south coast of England. Holidays had ranged from the Isle of Man to North Wales and the Lancashire coast, and apart from two years immediately after leaving college spent in

Gloucestershire and three in Smethwick, he had always lived in Lancashire. My mother's family had lived in the West Riding area of Saddleworth for 300 years, so I was a thorough-bred northerner. In Clitheroe, along with a standard of living much higher than that in Shaw, there was a cultural quality that was extremely attractive. I had many opportunities to enjoy intellectual interests with a number of professional people who were friendly and kind, and ministerial colleagues accepted the first woman minister on the scene without demur. Even though the vicar of Clitheroe disapproved, as a High Anglican, he and his wife were my good friends, and relations between the churches, including the Roman Catholics, were excellent. Nowhere else have I found such satisfaction of this sort.

The date eludes me, but one occasion was unforgettable. It was Good Friday and for the first time the Roman Catholics joined the rest of us in the parish church, making a congregation of some six to seven hundred. The Roman Catholic priest, three Anglicans, the Methodist minister and I stood and sat together and, during the service, sang with deep conviction, 'Thy love unknown has broken every barrier down'. The Rector of Stonyhurst College, run by Jesuits, began a memorable address with the words, 'Brothers and sisters in Christ'. Later, we strolled out into the gentle April evening - the moon shone high above Pendle Hill and in that quiet hour it was easy to think, 'God's in his heaven' and all is well. It was very good to belong to the Ribble Valley Council of Churches just as it was very good to be a minister of the United Reformed Church in Clitheroe, Newton and Barrow.

Did all this experience qualify me for a move to the affluent south and in particular to the renowned church at Purley? For too long I had championed the underprivileged and scorned those who had everything. My stepmother who had moved with me to Clitheroe, where she died, had often accused me of thinking the rich people of this world didn't need saving, I was so concerned for the poor. The stories of my father's poverty-stricken childhood, the dreary inadequate houses of the unemployed in Shaw, the suicides of men 'thrown on the scrap heap' in the '30s had certainly burned into my mind and heart. How could I ever adjust to Purley, whose reputation had reached the north as one of the most distinguished churches in the Congregational denomination. Pringle of Purley was as well known as Pringle of Scotland. In any case, at my age what could I offer? Wasn't it time I sat down and put my feet up?

That was not how I saw the situation. There was no reason for leaving Clitheroe as far as the church was concerned; I felt I could continue happily there, say for another two years, but Joyce's plea for me to move nearer the family was more than reasonable and to me it looked as if God was opening the way for me to do so and at the same time offering me an opportunity to work and be independent financially. So in May 1975 I left Clitheroe, once again to face a future I could never have guessed. Friends in Clitheroe gave me a unique present to take with me. Mr Hill the architect had been in Lebanon on business and had brought back a lovely gold chain for his wife and I had admired it. So he designed an exquisite gold cross with a similar chain and went to the gold market in Beirut where a Muslim created a unique gold cross for a Christian woman minister. It is of course priceless.

Sometimes at London committees I'd been asked, 'Where do you come from?' and the questioner, hearing I came from Lancashire, would say, 'But you haven't got a Lancashire accent!' I'd often thought southerners expected Lancastrians to wear clogs and have cotton sticking in their hair. A Scots accent seems to be generally acceptable if not desirable, but northern English accents are often regarded as 'common' or 'vulgar'. Once having decided that God had opened the way for me again, I didn't stop to think too much about the changes I would find in Purley. I said I would miss the hills: there are far more hills in Purley than Clitheroe, but they're covered with houses. I also said to myself, 'People are people wherever they are and surely I ought to be able to help Cyril Franks a bit.' I forgot what my stepmother had said about my lack of concern for the salvation of those who aren't poor, but I soon had to address myself to that question.

Chapter 12

Can Purley be saved?

On May 14, 1975, I had my last meal in Clitheroe with the neighbour who had given me my first meal on arrival there nine years previously, and drove south to spend the first night at Joyce and John's home on the Brighton Road in Purley. Just before midnight there was a road accident immediately in front of the house. John dashed out. A pedestrian had been killed. Although I was not involved in the drama I wondered what sort of a place I'd come to. It took me at least six months to get used to the traffic and find my way around. I soon discovered that I had moved a long long way from the comparatively leisurely pace of north-east Lancashire.

Beaumont Road was a quiet cul-de-sac and my manse was the last house, backing on to woodlands and Reedham School. The area is quite different now, since the sale of Reedham and its replacement with luxury homes. I didn't start working in Purley until June 1975 and was inducted on Saturday, June 28. A number of friends came down from Clitheroe, everybody was very kind, and as happens so often the details of the day were so absorbing that it was only later that I began to think very seriously about the charge I had received. Bernard Thorogood, then a member of Purley United Reformed Church and General Secretary of the Council for World Mission, addressed me and the church with the question, 'Can Purley be saved?' I hardly understood the question then, and 14 years later I'm not sure of the answer!

Bernard explained that he did not mean, 'We are in the race for conversions as junior competitors of the Baptists round the corner.' He meant, 'Can Purley be healed? Can Purley be made holy? Can Purley see the glory of life? Can Purley have hopes for the future and for all eternity?' He went on to point out the affluence of Purley which had shocked him when he returned from overseas, but admitted how easily he adjusted to comfort and privilege. He reminded us how hard it is for those who are lapped in privilege to enter the kingdom of God, and continued, 'So for our ministry here and for Kathleen in particular today, will you help us to sit lightly to all the comforts of an affluent society? Will you help us to be open to radical change? Will you show us what it means to live simply?' Community and hope were words that figured in the following paragraphs; then came this personal word, 'Kathleen, you come to us after lots of experience in a very different part of the country. Please don't become a Purley-ite too easily. Please keep your northern humour and commonsense and directness. Laugh at our pretensions. Perhaps you are called here and sent to us by the Spirit to complement Cyril's gifts.' The elders were so impressed and maybe chastened by this charge that they discussed it at length after it had been printed.

I had a lot of ideas about affluence. I had always accepted the fact that my mother's family were wealthy and well educated. My father had millionaire friends in the Isle of Man whom I had known and frequently visited from childhood. My first church treasurer and his wife were very rich and very generous people and in the short period of my marriage our standard of living had been high. Yet overnight my state had dropped from supertax, a chauffeur and gardener, two maids and two cars, and it hadn't hurt me very much to stay in the same house with one maid and one small car and a stipend of £400 per year. Hadn't St Paul learned to be content in whatsoever state he was? Hadn't we always been poor relations in the family? Yes, my stepmother was right – I was biased towards the poor and had been furious when I had heard a woman who lived in great luxury tell a fellow church member how to manage to keep house for herself and her husband on twenty-seven shillings per week.

Yet Purley's affluence hit me and shocked me. As my first Christmas approached, Cyril asked me to arrange a Nativity service and I requested a spotlight over the crib, thinking of a bulb on a flex, perhaps fixed in Heath Robinson fashion. At the next elders' meeting, the treasurer said, "I hear Kathleen has asked for a light for the Nativity service. We've talked for ages about improving the lighting in the chancel. If you will agree to the spending of £600, I can see to it tomorrow.' Without further discussion the elders agreed. Never had I asked for so little and got so much, but I was soon to find that Purley is like that. The church can and does produce tremendous sums of money most generously;

on the other hand people don't seem to leave large sums to the church in their wills. The standard of giving in freewill offerings is no higher per member than in some less affluent churches, and Purley does not readily respond to things like the 1% Appeal for World Development. Yet in an emergency incredible sums are given, and no minister in the denomination has been treated more generously than I have by Purley.

What I discovered in Purley must also be true of other affluent areas. Purley is suburbia and, as Bernard Thorogood pointed out, lacks a sense of community such as I had known in Clitheroe. As he put it, 'Salvation has to do with community and Purley doesn't have much of that.' Commuters who get up early in the morning to beat rush hour traffic to London and return maybe at seven in the evening can, I think, be forgiven for retreating to their secluded homes and gardens with no enthusiasm to turn out for 8 pm church and elders' meetings and numerous committees. Many a time I have appreciated and admired the considerable number of Purley church members who have been willing to give up their hard-earned leisure to serve the Church.

One of the greatest assets of Purley United Reformed Church as I see it is its geographical position on the main road near the superstores and baths and hospital and post office; and if there is one thing more than another which the church does excellently it is providing weekday opportunities for people to meet and relax in a friendly atmosphere with a cup of coffee or a light meal. It is almost an ever-open door where people can and do drop in and often find help. I learned this very soon after my arrival when there was a minor road accident, and several people came in to wait for another car. They were in a state of slight shock and both Cyril and I were on hand to support them; and most days strangers as well as members of the congregation can find a minister or skilled lay people as well as a good church keeper on the premises if they have personal needs; and all sorts of enquiries are made about weddings, baptisms, financial help, accommodation and of course matrimonial problems.

This daily ministry does contribute something very valuable to hundreds of people in Purley. It is outreach to the community. It also provides opportunities for many church people to serve in ways in which they are competent. Retired men do a lot of work about the premises. Many people bake for the coffee service and cook for Friday lunches and organise the Thursday soup 'n' cheese lunch. There are those who look after the shoppers' creche – yes, all these activities go a long way to answering the question about community in Purley, and in addition there are the popular literary society and badminton and Scottish dancing which include in their membership a large number who are not church members. My church in Clitheroe had attempted community service on a smaller scale. Like Purley it was well placed in the centre of the town and had a number of links with the town, but it had not the resources in personnel or premises that exist in Purley. Sometimes northern friends, knowing how affluent the south is, have said to me, 'But do they care? Do they give their time?' and to those queries without hesitation I can say, 'Yes'.

Obviously one of the first things I had to learn in Purley was to play as part of a team, and there were those who doubted whether after 40 years of being in pastoral charge alone I could adapt. It could have been difficult but Cyril Franks made it very easy. From the beginning we were 'colleagues', not boss and assistant. True he carried ministerial responsibility more than I did and that suited me because I was already old and lucky to have the opportunity to work. One of the things Cyril found good in Purley was the freedom the church gave him to exercise the kind of ministry he felt he could and ought to do. In the same way Cyril himself let me do the things I felt I could do. But there was one big difference from ministry in Clitheroe with which I found it very difficult to come to terms. I had no previous experience of the Bible Belt!

At a Swanwick conference I had heard college principal Hubert Cunliffe Jones say that he hoped he would never grow too academic to sing the children's hymn 'Jesus loves me, this I know for the Bible tells me so', and it was a word I agreed with wholeheartedly. Bible criticism, linguistic studies, interest particularly in Hinduism and Islam – all had me fascinated, and critical. Experience of life in pastoral charge, working in a 'man's' world, Jim's death and Joyce's illness had all roused many questions and doubts. There were many occasions when I couldn't guess the future or see any light at the end of the tunnel, but I never lost completely the conviction that 'underneath were everlasting arms' nor the faith that 'nothing can separate us from the love of God which is in Christ Jesus'.

As a young schoolgirl in World War I, stories of angels at Mons left me sceptical, but when I heard Sir Ernest Shackleton lecture on his expedition to the Antarctic and then read his recorded diary, an indelible picture was fixed in my mind. Even then I could relate to his experience, of which he wrote, 'When I look back on those days I have no doubt that Providence guided us. I know that during that long and racking march of 36 hours over the unnamed mountains and glaciers it seemed to me often that we were four not three. I said nothing but afterwards Worsley said to me, "Boss, I had a curious feeling on the march that there was another person with us". Crean confessed to the same idea...'

One very dark wild night, driving my Austin Eight through torrential rain with two little girls asleep in the back, I was sad and lonely – it was soon after Jim's death. I was comforted by an unseen presence in the passenger seat beside me – Jim's ministering spirit? Otto's mysterium tremendum? Or the power so often spoken of by ordinary Lancashire folk who said, 'I never thought I could do it but when you need it somehow you're given strength.' Maybe a psychical research student in another generation will explain the experience. Like Shackleton (though never having been on any great physical adventure), time and again I have thought and felt God beside me. Recently I have heard of a young Czech scientist doing astro-physics becoming a Christian through his knowledge of matter and non-matter in spite of his atheistic upbringing; and one of our United Reformed Church ministers, Kate Compston, has written of the new interest of scientists in the spiritual dimension. I find this exciting.

My life is quite inexplicable to me apart from a spiritual dimension, or the leading of the Holy Spirit, and I cannot imagine any circumstance which would make me change my mind about these things; but I had long outgrown the simplistic Christianity advocated by the evangelicals I met when I came to Purley. I could not throw overboard the radical theology I had learned and I could not accept the Billy Graham style preoccupation with personal salvation which seemed to me self-centred rather than Christ-centred. Consequently it was a severe shock to me to find so many southerners enthusiastic about evangelism as they saw it in 'mission' experience. As Bernard Thorogood had said, salvation has to do with community and therefore the Church has to be concerned with the human situation and politics. Christian Aid, protests against injustice wherever found, wealth gained at the expense of the most vulnerable members of society – these are things I can't help being passionately concerned about even though most of the time there is so little I can do about them. If only I were 25 again and had the physique, I wouldn't be in Purley! But haven't I said, 'Purley is my God-given opportunity' and such ministry as I can render has to be with those for whom materially speaking, everything in the garden is lovely.

Yet everything in Purley is far from lovely, and during 14 years here I have found more personal and social problems than ever I knew in 50 years in Lancashire. When people are poor and have no alternatives they get on with life, usually with few complaints and great courage. Affluence makes life more complicated in all sorts of ways. I once asked a doctor friend how many lights his big Ford car had. My little Austin Eight had 13. He counted 29 and commented, 'Twenty-nine more things to go wrong'. My children in Shaw walked to the local primary school and then went on buses with their friends to the grammar school. They did not like me to meet them! In Purley mums have to ferry children to school, to Cubs, to Brownies, to dancing class, to football, to the swimming pool – in fact everywhere every day; and in the holidays they have to take them with them to the shops because there is no-one to leave them with at home. Is it any wonder that young women feel stressed? My son-in-law has said, we've got all the labour-saving gadgets that can go wrong, but we can't afford a maid.

There is a myth that Lancashire folk are open and friendly but southerners don't talk. My ministerial colleagues agree that people in the south do tell their troubles and discuss their problems and in many ways are very dependent on ministerial support. Again this could reflect a general change in society where, through the media, people are forever talking about themselves, their ailments, their bereavements, their urges, their age problems. Are people more demanding than they used to be? Are they more conscious of their rights? Does the cut and thrust of everday life make people more aggressive? Sometimes it seems so – perhaps people in the north today are different from those I knew years ago. It is strange now to remember how it was said that I adjusted to Purley very easily.

Away back in Shaw, the Crompton Musical Society had as its producer Hervey Rhodes. His wife Ann was a particular friend of mine – we had common interests. We both had two small daughters, we were both involved in the Guide movement. Hervey was a keen competitor with my uncle in the woollen trade in Delph only four miles away. He became Labour MP for Ashton-under-Lyne and was later knighted, but they both remained unspoiled and it was Lady Rhodes whom I found one night on her knees scrubbing the wooden floor of a house given to Oldham Guides. As a member of the Board of Trade and an expert on the Sudan and trade with China, Hervey gave up part of an Easter vacation to come and talk to my youth club about the cotton trade. By the time I went to Clitheroe he was Lord Lieutenant of Lancashire, although he lived just over the border in Yorkshire. I had only been in Purley a few weeks when I received an invitation from the Rhodes to go to a party at the House of Lords. When I replied I asked what kind of dress I should wear and got a note from Hervey saying, 'Come in your cassock'. It was, so to speak, a royal command and on a lovely summer evening I took the train and then a taxi to the House of Lords wearing my cassock. Socially it was the most exciting night of my life. Very well-known people from both Houses were there including the Speaker, the Prime Minister, the Liberal leader and of course many friends from other walks of life. During the evening not only did the Speaker discuss Methodist lay preaching with me and a rabbi talk about the first woman to be ordained as a rabbi, but in his familiar blunt way, Hervey said to the Prime Minister, 'Harold, I want you to meet Kathleen. She's a minister in the United Reformed Church.'

It was only after the party that I got to know it was the occasion of Hervey and Ann's Golden Wedding. They were a wonderful pair and loyal good friends. Their interest followed me and my family in Purley until Hervey died in 1987. I last visited him in his ninety-first year when he had just returned from his fifth visit to China. I cannot imagine what my father would have said had he known I had been to the House of Lords – and had been invited to conduct worship at the City Temple, which he had talked about so often when I was a student.

After one year in Purley the unexpected happened again. Cyril Franks was invited to be moderator of the Southern Province and decided to accept the challenge. When I first came to Purley they accepted me believing that Cyril was 'in charge' and I doubt if at that time the church would have taken kindly to any suggestion that it should submit to the full leadership of a woman. To be number one minister at Purley was a very important job. Some actually said that after Purley a minister could not possibly move to another pastoral charge, and that was why Purley had already produced two other moderators. In 1976 Cyril and Joan Franks moved and transferred their membership to Sanderstead, and Purley was left with me. When the District Council considered the appointment of an interim moderator Purley answered, 'We've got Kathleen' and the District acquiesced. So a 70-year-old woman had responsibility, at least temporarily, for Purley United Reformed Church. There followed a difficult 14 months. For years schemes had been prepared and rejected and new ones brought forward for alterations to the buildings. It was generally agreed that the premises needed to be more open to the public. Other facilities were overdue, but obviously changes of that magnitude were not going to be made during a vacancy. All I felt I could or should do was to keep things ticking over until the coming of a new leader.

At a meeting of the Maintainance of the Ministry Committee in the summer of 1977 I met John Waller, then ministering in Derby and secretary to the Derby District. He asked one question about the relationship that would exist between us if he were to come to Purley. I assured him that he could have all the responsibility; I was long past wishing to be 'the boss'. From that day John and I had a very good understanding as colleagues and a friendship that is still invaluable. He and his wife Margaret with their children Simon and Katie came to Purley in the autumn of '77. On the day they arrived my daughter Joyce invited them across the road for a meal and the four children got on so well together that Simon and Katie stayed on in the afternoon. They were respectively one year older than Bruce and Sheena. I took them all to the cinema that day. Soon afterwards they formed 'a gang' and enjoyed dozens of hours together. It soon became apparent that Purley had been guided by God's spirit to call John Waller to its ministry. He had the gifts that were most needed at that time and under his leadership some of the long-cherished dreams and plans became realities.

Shaw never had the scope for two ministers, and certainly could never have afforded two, but soon after I went there in 1931, a retired minister and his wife came to live in the town. He was the Revd C W Clarke who had just retired from Delph. He had been Minister in Shaw for 14 years at the beginning of the century. Strangely, he had conducted my mother's funeral in Delph and had known of my grandfather. He was a very good preacher and still had a magnificent voice when he came back to Shaw as a septuagenarian. I loved to hear his stories of my independent-minded grandfather, who had left the Anglican Church in Delph because he could not stand the ritual and joined the Methodists; but decided they were also conformists so went off to the Independent chapel, which was Congregational, 200 yards away. There he got into trouble because the congregation refused burial to a suicide and padlocked the gates against her coffin. My grandfather smashed the gates with a mallet and buried the girl himself in the Independent churchyard. I gathered that Mr Clarke had a lot of sympathy for him. Quite often when I was on holiday or at another church Shaw would invite Mr Clarke to conduct Sunday worship, which he did most effectively. He had more than 40 years experience behind him and I was an inexperienced beginner but he insisted on saying he was 'my little piecer'. In the cotton spinning mills the 'little piecer' was the lowliest beginner – it was his task to mend any threads that broke in the spinning process and there was quite a knack in doing that.

When John Waller became the minister of Purley, I often thought of myself as the 'little piecer'. It was not my job to direct or initiate policies and I did not carry much responsibility. Because John was a first class colleague we shared equally in the conduct of worship and I for the most part 'did as I was told' during the week. Obviously the time had come when leadership had passed out of my hands and that caused me no regrets. I realised how very fortunate I was to be able to work in a happy situation and to have a home of my own so near my family. Unlike so many others, ministers have fairly flexible working hours. Consequently I could pick up Bruce and Sheena from school and have them for tea regularly. In the school holidays I could take a day off to show them some of the great sights of London. Once they visited a patient in Guy's Hospital with me and then we went off to the Tower on a lovely summer afternoon. They also provided me with children's addresses from time to time, like the occasion when we visited the Planetarium and listened to the story of the stars, and Sheena whispered, 'Granny, was God there then?'

When Jim died, I never dreamed that one day there would be Bruce, and I parted with most of Jim's possessions. But I kept a model yacht made to scale for him and when I came to Purley handed it over to Bruce. We found it leaked and a friend interested in boats offered to look at it. The wood had dried out but the yacht was soon restored to pristine condition. When Bruce went with me to collect it he was told what a very lucky boy he was to own such a splendid craft – it was worth hundreds of pounds. On the way home in the car Bruce said, 'Granny, when you die and go to heaven will you see my grandpa?' I hoped I would. Then he said, 'Will you please tell him I've got his boat.' That day and on many other occasions I wished tremendously that the children could have known Jim – how he would have delighted in them. But had he lived, I would never have come to Purley. Time heals wounds, though after tragic loss life is never the same again.

The routine of Purley was very different from that of Shaw and

Clitheroe and I had never previously had experience of a church relationship with an inner city community like the one between Purley and Crossway Mission at the Elephant and Castle in London. At first it bewildered me to see Purley people serving tea in Crown Derby china cups at their magnificent houses with swimming pools in Silver Lane to thoroughgoing Londoners. Was I seeing new Ladies Bountiful? Didn't the visitors resent Purley's luxurious living? I soon found out that there was genuine friendship between these unlikely groups – they really knew each other individually and the Purley women regularly visited homes in the concrete jungle. I was never sure that such a relationship could develop with the younger generation. Before Purley, I had known and lived in comparatively small communities with populations of about twelve thousand. They were mixed communities and most of the people knew each other. In Shaw the road on which we lived, and on which my church stood, housed two bank managers, two doctors, several mill 'bosses' and teachers. Opposite to our house there was a small pub frequented by none of these people, but by the neighbours nearby, who included a disreputable drunken sailor with a consequently shabby family, a very respectable churchgoing family employed in domestic service and the habitual burglar I've already mentioned, who lived directly opposite the Chairman of the Bench. We all knew each other! Nowadays there are 'harvest home' luxury complexes for the elderly, very poor quality high rise flats for those who cannot afford anything better, classy estates in the stockbroker belts, and cardboard boxes for the homeless. Sometimes the old situations I knew, with all their faults, seem like another world. One thing is certain, human problems in Purley are at least as numerous and horrific as any I knew in Lancashire.

Chapter 13

Reaching out, moving out

1979 began badly for my family. In January John my son-in-law had a heart attack and after leaving intensive care in Mayday Hospital, Croydon, had a second which might have been fatal had he not still been in hospital. John Waller gave me leave of absence and himself helped considerably to support Joyce who inevitably had to shoulder very heavy responsibilities. Thanks to the advances of medicine, unlike Jim 30 years earlier, John has mercifully survived but there were days when I dreaded history repeating itself.

During the same year I had an interesting new experience as interim moderator at Banstead, when I made many friends. Although only five miles away, Banstead is very different for Purley. It is a village community, and the church was approaching its golden jubilee. It is smaller in size and in numbers than Purley, but is strong and affluent and, like Purley, has an international link with West Germany.

Purley's Partnership experience is an interesting feature of its life. Back in the days of the International Congregational Council I had not only been in Hartford, Connecticut, but had met several church leaders from the Rhineland Palatinate where church relations had been fostered after the end of World War II. I discovered that Purley had actually got a relationship with Hartford Cyril Franks having been there on an exchange, and Hartford's Bob and Sally Edwards having many friends in Purley. I had met them in 1958. By the time I arrived in Purley, there was a close partnership between Speyer in the Palatinate, Hartford and Purley. At first I was not in the least impressed because it looked to me like a rich man's club enjoyed by a fairly small group in Purley United Reformed Church. There were great triennial gatherings rotating between the three countries, in Hartford in 1977 and in Purley in 1980. During the years however the Partnership has widened and caring has deepened, thanks to the vision and hard work of John Waller and others, so that by 1989 the partnership included not only churches in the USA, England and West Germany, but East Germany (Dessau) and Czechoslovakia (Ostrava), with a strong link in Belfast.

The Irish connection began when children came over for a holiday in Purley and it developed later when the Revd Andrew Lorimer came with his family to Walton-on-the-Hill where they were able to live in the manse while Andrew qualified for the URC roll of ministers and looked after the Walton church. With characteristic generosity several people in Purley helped to finance the Lorimers until they had established their independence and during that period I learned a great deal about the tensions in Northern Ireland as I spent study hours with Andrew. John Waller had to exercies tremendous patience and perseverance in making a relationship with the Presbyterian church in Belfast. At first there was a considerable amount of suspicion about Purley's motives, which I have always been convinced are good, though sometimes I did feel a little unease about existing partnerships between churches. I do not question the sincerity, goodwill and friendship that exists between a number of families, and the pleasure gained from meeting together, but I sometimes wonder if a church like Purley could be as interested in a city in this country which is in great need but is less exciting.

Nominally there is a link between Purley and Roundshaw, which is nearly on Purley's doorstep but a totally different place. When I first came to Purley the ministers at the Roundshaw ecumenical project were Keith and Dorothy Spence who were friends of mine. I had a sense of guilt about their situation. I didn't know how to help them nor how Purley could do much for them. Recently a young minister confessed that a relationship with a European church isn't very exciting now that we are all involved in Europe and he longed for twinning with a place in the Far East to which visits could be made. Purley's relationship with Northern Ireland is more tenuous than with Germany and it is more difficult to make a positive contribution to that situation where the need is at least as great and maybe our Christian responsibility is greater. I suspect that where outreach is most desperately needed we are all inadequate to give it. Having said that, I confess Purley's connection with Dessau had become very interesting to me. Thinking

I might go there I joined an elementary German class in the autumn of 1987. I did not become proficient but at least words became recognisable.

The following spring, Peter and Hilary Baily invited me to go with them on a private visit to Dessau in May, and arranged to take me 'door to door' by car to stay with Pfarrer Wolfgang Steckel and his wife Sigrid. Before we left Purley, one member of the Partnership Committee said, 'Kathleen, I'm green with envy.' After lovely warm days at home we arrived in Dessau in cold drizzling rain. The church was swathed in plastic sheeting and was closed; the town looked grey and poverty-sticken even by old Lancashire standards. The manse showed signs of financial strain and I wondered at first why on earth anyone should be green with envy about my visit. Within 24 hours I knew why. Dessau 'got me'.

True, we had to report to the police on a very wet morning. True, there was virtually no fruit in the shops and there were queues for fresh meat and fresh bread; but the people were so welcoming, so open, so very much on our wavelength that the language barrier did not matter, and in a few days I learned a lot and got some surprises. On Sunday morning all over the town church bells called people to worship. As we gathered with Herr Steckel's congregation he asked me to voice greetings from Purley. It was Whit Sunday and once again we all understood each other and recognised God's presence together. When serving Communion, Herr Steckel asked if I would serve him with bread and wine. I was dressed in holiday clothes – no matter; and suddenly without any forethought at all, having given him the elements, I kissed him. The congregation got the message: East and West were reconciled and were made one in Christ. That morning none of us dreamed that in less than two years the Berlin Wall would go down and Eastern Europe would be free. Sigrid was still longing to be an old age pensioner so that she could come to Purley; she did not think the way would open before then! How often it has happened that we have been outpaced by God. How often we have prayed hardly expecting our prayers to be answered!

When I came to Purley in 1975 Bernard Thorogood said I brought with me considerable experience. It was true, but I came to a very different work situation especially in regard to ecumenical relations. How often I have longed to be back with the Ribble Valley Council of Churches. It hurt to hear Purley referred to time and again as 'the four parishes', with constant reminders that the Anglican church calendar had always to be a top priority. The lack of commitment to real unity all but destroyed my eagerness for cooperation. Fifteen years on I am happy to say the situation has improved and there is more concern for Purley Churches Together.

Inside Purley URC I had to get used to much more weekday activity than I had ever known before. This resulted from the fact that Purley has at its disposal a great many men and women who have time to give to the church during the week as well as considerable skills and willingness to work for the church. The thriving Diners' Club catered for young adults too old for the youth club, and very soon older people started Second Sitting – that meant social gatherings and meals in various homes. These occasions not only provided friendship for church members but sometimes introduced people from outside or on the fringes to come into the church, just as regular coffee mornings and lunches have done. There are many ways of evangelism and outreach, and just as a pantomime in Shaw saved Alice for the church, so a Saturday party with sherry and a glass of wine has opened up the way for others. My son-in-law once told me that he found cocktail parties opportunities where people talked to him about religion. If God is involved in all our living, people like me must never neglect or despise the opportunities given to us to pass on our faith – and the opportunities in Purley are very different from the ones I'd known previously.

One wintry afternoon in 1948 in the days of the London Missionary Society I trudged in wellies through snow for a mile to address a women's meeting on missionary work. There was no chairman and no pianist. I was asked to go ahead and do what was needed. At the end of my address dear Miss Howarth, a retired confectioner, stood up and said, 'We five on the front row are all over 75 – I am the youngest. We are all stone deaf so we haven't heard a word you have said, but we do thank you for coming.' The rest of the elderly audience then joined her to sing 'From Greenland's icy mountains... they call us to deliver their land'. As I trudged home in the gathering darkness that February day my thoughts on mission were as depressing as the weather. Forty years on I sit in comfort and hear desperate cries and see men, women and children dying for lack of water, food and shelter in many places. I also see doctors, nurses and many skilled volunteers trying to rescue them. I see a government official fly out to a disaster area, carrying in her plane a million water purifying tablets, and babies' vests and old people's blankets wrapped round medical supplies – and still the aid doesn't match the need. Sometimes today's help seems as ineffective as that small meeting in 1948. Yet the work of outreach with changing methods goes on and in spite of inadequacy I still believe God calls us to share in the monumental task of building his kingdom on earth in every possible way.

Before retiring I had opportunities to share the gospel in Purley that didn't exist in my previous churches to the same extent. In serious Bible study it was sheer joy to share information about the Old and New Testament texts alongside John Waller who also led study groups. He was a first-rate historian and between us I think we opened up the Scriptures for a number of interested learners.

In 1981 I was still coping with full-time work, going to Manchester to the college education committee and governors' meetings and taking part in assessment conferences. The regular services of worship at Purley, John and I shared equally; whichever of us preached also drew up the order of service, choosing readings and hymns and prayers. The one who did not preach usually did the talk to the children, which some grown-ups admitted they enjoyed more than the sermons. Although I suspected this was often true, the fact dismayed me. Purley boasted so many 'top' people in business and education; they had been served by distinguished ministers for years. Did it mean the hour of worship was simply a time of relaxation when they did not need to use their brains vigorously? Since I have retired there have been many changes in the patterns of worship and at least some of them demand cerebral concentration.

Our Thursday lunch-time services drew bigger congregations from several churches than Sunday evening worship did. The dramatic society was active. My own particular joy was, however, Sunday morning's music. Away back in Shaw the fairly large evening congregation had always been ready to 'make a joyful noise to the Lord' but the standard of organ music had often been abysmal and a choir non-existent. Voluntaries before and after worship and during the offertory ranged from 'The Yellow Rose of Texas', to the 'Z-cars' theme with sometimes a rendering of Handel's 'Largo'. One of my teacher friends had tried hard to help me with a junior choir and provided a lot of 'reasonable' music for me, but I was no expert myself. Late in my second ministry at Shaw, Dr Berriman and his family joined the church and he became organist. He created a small choir and introduced Bach chorales as voluntaries, all of which cheered me enormously, but the siting and condition of the church organ made it quite impossible for good quality church music to be developed. Things at Clitheroe were much better. There was a competent choir, but the organ was not very good. So when I came to Purley and found a well-trained robed choir, a pleasant junior choir and an able and very co-operative organist, worship really took on a new dimension for me. The final sung Amen used by Brian Allaker often seemed to me to rise straight to heaven as a paean of praise.

By the end of the summer of 1982 I had decided that I ought to stop working full-time, and so suggested to John Waller that I become half-time assistant. At first he was reluctant to accept the idea and asked if there was no chance that I might change my mind. Finally it was agreed by church meeting that I worked half time. The arrangement between me and John was 'flexible' and on at least one occasion he said, 'Everybody knows there are eight days in the week, and Kathleen has Wednesday off.' We were both content, I think. I certainly was, but obviously 'the writing was on the wall'. The arrangements would not continue very long and in any case I was 76.

The *Croydon Advertiser* made my decision to retire known with the headline, 'At 77, Kathleen calls it a day'. Time and again I had begged Joyce to tell me if she heard the least whisper that I was past it. In the event I did not need telling. I realised that I could not do justice to another winter's work, so asked to be taken off the payroll at the end of August 1983. I had not the money to buy a house, and was most grateful to the United Reformed Church for allowing me to find accommodation which the Retired Ministers' Housing Association would buy, and for which I could pay a small rent. After looking at many properties, the day I found the maisonette in Mitchley Avenue on the edge of Purley and Sanderstead, I knew at once that was the right home for me.

Purley gathered together an enormous sum to provide an annuity for me. The very thought of their generosity is still breathtaking.

Chapter 14

Fourscore years - and some sorrow

On holiday in the Scillies I once picked up a plaque with the message, 'How beautiful it is to do nothing and then rest afterwards'.

On pastoral visits I thought I had learned a lot about retirement: I had listened to those who enjoyed it and to those who did not. Some found so much to do they could not think how they had ever had time to work, and others seemed to do nothing day after day, week in week out. One of my friends complained that when she was working she had not the time to enjoy herself, but when she retired she had not the money to do all the things she wanted to do. How many times had I heard, 'I don't want to be a burden!' 'I want to stay independent as long as possible!' On the other hand there was the woman who insisted, 'I've got two daughters, one does my shopping and the other does my washing – it's their duty isn't it? We've brought them up!' I wanted to do things my way as long as possible, though Joyce tried to persuade me that there are people who like to be dependent and enjoy being looked after. Obviously I had to recognise the fact that I could only continue alone with the background support of family and friends.

I had to re-adjust my relationship with Purley United Reformed Church, and fortunately had no regrets in relinquishing responsiblity there. It was very pleasant not to feel duty bound to attend meetings and do visits. It soon became clear that there were opportunities in the district to conduct Sunday worship in various churches, and although nothing equals the privilege of regular worship with one's own congregation, it became a delight to have lots of time to write new sermons and get to know other churches. Retirement also brought more time for entertaining friends. I have found it almost impossible to make people believe I am not terrifically busy all the time. I always could enjoy idleness and as time goes by I like it more and more. Living alone almost inevitably produces self-indulgence and selfishness because there's no-one to question my right to do what I want, to eat what I want, to watch what I want, to get up and go to bed when I want. This can be compensation for 'losing' one's family.

As a child I had piano lessons but never achieved very high standards. I had always been interested in hymns and other church music and had kept my piano. After some months of retirement I screwed up courage to ask a teacher in Purley United Reformed Church if she would consider giving me lessons. She had never taken on an 'oldie' before but agreed to have me, and that has proved a most beneficial experience. It means learning new things: concentrating my mind for something like an hour a day and exercising my fingers and hands – all of which has proved enjoyable as well as useful.

Six years have gone by quickly, for the most part happily, but one of the penalties of longevity is the loss of contemporaries by death, by removal to distant homes and by other limitations on mobility.

In 1984 after visiting Lancashire by car in the spring, I went to Toronto in the autumn to spend a month with Barbara, Jimmy and Jeremy. They had a pleasant situation at Port Credit where we were able to have a family gathering with cousins from Ottawa and my stepbrother and family from Toronto. The time passed all too quickly.

The church in Shaw with which I celebrated its golden jubilee in 1935 reached its centenary in July 1985 and the secretary asked if I would preach. Joyce went with me for the weekend celebrations. She gathered a number of the 'old youth group' for a Saturday night party and we all managed to walk in the procession on the Sunday afternoon to hold a short open air service where it had all begun 100 years earlier. The morning service was recorded on a videotape. That weekend was a very great highlight in my long ministry. It is wonderful to see and hear people 50 years on; remembering them as babies you have baptised, teenagers you have played with in the youth club, couples you have married, and some stalwarts of the early years happy to have grown old still in the service of Shaw church. As one member remarked, the Church is the only institution to which the whole family can belong from 'the cradle to the grave'. To share in Shaw's centenary was both humbling and satisfying.

Unfortunately I was conscious of Jim's absence – and of Barbara's, but she at least had been over at Easter and we had visited Shaw together.

In 1985 John Waller left Purley to become moderator of the West Midlands Province, and it was not until September 1986 that the Revd Raymond Adams returned from service in Taiwan and was inducted to the pastoral charge of Purley. For the first time for more than 50 years I was just a member of the congregation, but it wasn't long before there developed a very good relationship between me and the new minister and his family, who were actually younger than my own daughter and her family. Early in 1987 the Manchester High School Old Girls' Federation in London invited me to speak at their annual lunch about my life and work in the ministry. Because of college and other interests, I had never been a 'good' member of the Old Girls' Federation and did not expect to know anybody at the lunch, but John Waller had persuaded me that I ought to put on record my experience in the ministry and I saw the High School's invitation as an opportunity to try out a potted account of my life and work on an unknown audience who were not church-based. Many old High School women in London have distinguished careers. If they should find my story interesting maybe others would, especially as the question of the ministry of women in the Anglican Church was hitting the headlines. In the event what I had to say was so well received it encouraged me to start this autobiography.

On July 9 1988 Bruce, my grandson, had his twentieth birthday and with two student friends he was ready to go to Africa. A carefully planned but hazardous adventure would take them from Nairobi across Uganda and Zaire, by canoe down the Congo river to Kinshasa, then back to Nairobi. They were to fly to Nairobi the next day, Sunday. On that Saturday morning about 9.30 there was an SOS call from Caterham United Reformed Church. The minister wasn't well - could I possibly take Sunday morning's service? As I sat preparing it, Raymond Adams phoned to say that a greatly-loved elder and friend in Purley had died; his wife's parents were members at Caterham. Later in the day Joyce phoned to say John, my son-in-law, had suffered what might be a stroke. Could I go as soon as possible after the service at Caterham?

When I drove to their home in Chipstead what would I find? In the event I was immediately greeted by 30 young people just departing from the birthday party. John was up and dressed though obviously stricken – his consultant was expected soon. An excellent Sunday lunch appeared, enhanced with exciting conversation by Bruce's friends. Bruce himself was even quieter than usual. Should he pull out from the African trip? He was to be the party's first-aider and had been briefed by Joyce. Ought he to leave home not knowing how his father's illness might develop? He delayed packing to the latest possible moment, but eventually the three took off. Later John went into hospital; ever since, sadly, he has been very limited in physical movement.

Sheena was 18 on August 2 and, following her brother Bruce's pattern, she arranged a fairly large party of family and friends. On August 1, however, at 6 am there was a phone call from Calgary to say that my daughter Barbara was in a coma and not expected to live. She had emigrated to Canada with her husband and son Jeremy several years earlier and I had been out to see them there. Very shortly I heard that Barbara had died, and as the funeral was to be immediate her ex-husband did not wish me to go to Calgary. I hadn't known Barbara was ill. As was her wont, she sometimes phoned frequently and then weeks would go by and she would not communicate. What a lot had happened in one short month! Over long years, professionally and personally I had learned to cope with crises and sorrow. In old age it was inevitable that contemporaries would disappear. I was quite sure nothing would hurt me as much as the loss of Jim, though I had agonised deeply over Joyce's illness; but it seemed quite unnatural for a daughter to die before me.

Barbara had always learned the hard way, but she was very lovable and I had loved her deeply. Sometimes John had told me I was the one sure anchor in her life and on one occasion when I had cried in despair, 'Where have I failed?' John had answered, 'One only fails when one stops loving'. I not only grieved for myself but I was very sad to see John seriously handicapped, Joyce heavily burdened and Jeremy motherless. Being old I was on the sidelines, able to do little or nothing, and I realised that I had not been there when Barbara was born, nor when she was married, nor when she died but she was my dear daughter.

In September Joyce invited me to go with her to Sligachan on Skye. As we were about to leave there was a phone-call from the British Embassy in Kinshasa, the capital of Zaire. There had been an accident on the river. The last we had heard from Bruce was over a month previously. They were about to buy a dug-out canoe and set off down the river. We all knew that there were dangers involved in such an expedition, but no-one had reckoned with a cargo boat smashing into the canoe during the night, splitting it in two and spilling all its contents into the river. There were no further details. There was no word of how they had coped with the dangers, obtaining enough food and drinking water, avoiding swarms of mosquitoes and finding safe places for their hammocks in the dense jungle of the river bank. We could not hear their stories of the places they had visited and the people they had met. It was a fortnight later, on John's birthday, September 17, that the whole story was revealed, when the three friends at last flew in from Nairobi. God surely had heard prayers for the safety of those three students and we were spared a further family tragedy.

The mountains and the storms over Skye, the rainbow spanning the Cuillin Hills, the quiet and Joyce's company all contributed to restoring my faith and confidence, but it was only at the end of September that I began to think again about the future and gave up a lot of self-pity. Bruce phoned to ask if he and Sheena could come for an evening meal so that he could tell me of his African adventure. They arrived at about 4.30 pm and I heard first-hand about the accident on the Congo. The cargo boat was travelling with minimal lighting at half past midnight and did not stop after sinking the canoe and all their belongings. They swam to the river edge and after clinging to tree branches swam further down-river till they came to a small mud bank onto which they clambered, spending the next four hours crouched in shock in the still, chilly darkness. They had lost everything except their lives and the scant clothes they wore. A fisherman then paddled by and took them to his hut until much later a boat, skippered by a minister, stopped and took them back in the direction they had come. They had canoed 900 kilometres and had been within 100 kilometres of their goal.

After five days on the boat they were brought to a forestry plantation where some French and Portuguese were working. They took care of them and eventually flew them on their weekly supply plane to Kinshasa. There the consul was waiting for them on the airstrip. He had booked them in at a hotel, but decided instead to take them to his own villa for the weekend. Then an Embassy official lent them his flat for a week until money could be sent from England and arrangements made for them to be flown to Nairobi, where Sudan Air accepted their story and replaced their return tickets to England. I think it said a great deal for the three of them that people believed their story and treated them so well.

Prior to the accident, Bruce had been deeply impressed by the kind generosity and friendliness of Africans in mud huts who had rarely seen white people before. He told me of the drums that passed word on about their coming, of days without food, of the river water they had to drink, giving rise to regular bouts of diarrhoea, despite Joyce's tablets. Villagers would accept no payment for hospitality – only maybe for a chicken. They received Oxfam clothing, which they gave back before leaving. The minister/captain bought them 'flip-flops' for their bare feet. They were taken to church where theirs were the only white faces and they were made to sit very conspicuously at the front. Bruce had to read the lesson from I Kings 17, the story of Elijah and the widow's cruse of oil and handful of meal, and, much to their embarrassment, the minister preached that God had sent the village three modern-day Elijahs! In one place children screamed in terror at their approach because they had been told white men eat babies...

It was fascinating to listen to Bruce and there were a thousand more details I longed to hear. The saddest fact was that Bruce's excellent photos and diary were at the bottom of the Congo river. The visit gave me much to ponder, and made me proud of Bruce, who was already thinking about the next adventure. Jim would have shared the thrill of his grandson – especially as Bruce has followed him in Scouting and that night left me to go and tell the Venture Scouts about his travels.

The phone rang – could John Waller come and stay a night next week on his trip to the moderators' meeting in London? Yes, I was beginning to look forward and think maybe I need not feel quite useless. Life was getting back to normal after three dramatic months which convinced me – if I needed convincing – that stagnation was not the order of the day for my retirement.

Chapter 15

Life goes on

1989 and a New Year. What could it bring for an octogenarian? In the old days on New Year's Eve there had always been church parties followed by Watchnight services which ended at midnight with lots of kisses and good wishes for the New Year. Once, in what now seems another life, I dashed home after a Watchnight service to meet Jim waiting for me with a beautiful diamond ring that had both our initials and the date engraved on the inside. It was in the first hour of that New Year we became officially engaged. Consequently New Year celebrations have always held a special significance for me – a secret happiness. Fifty-two years later what could a New Year bring? One thing for sure, springtime, which is always most delightful in Purley with so much colour and new life that it lifts one's spirit to go down the tree-lined roads with pink and white, yellow and purple blossoms and fresh green leaves. In springtime, Purley is at its best and with all the natural evidence of life I never feel it is hard to believe in Resurrection here. I have often wondered how one can relate autumn to Easter in the southern hemisphere.

In January 1989 neither I nor anybody else anticipated the revolutionary events in Europe that were to come before the end of the year, and with my usual failure to guess right I never imagined that the year would bring me many 'first time' experiences – but it did. I read a financial article in a daily newspaper which began, 'Widows are often seen as frail old ladies who devote their twilight years to knitting.' By 1989 I was getting accustomed to some people treating me as though I was fragile, in need of a supporting arm; a person who should be addressed as 'luv' or 'dear' by bus drivers and shop assistants, or worse still, somebody who could not be expected to understand documents or even money. Sometimes I found such attitudes impertinent and hard to tolerate; but how much better old age can be today than in the old days - if one was lucky enough to survive the Biblical 'three score years and ten'! What a difference has been made to the quality of later living by dentures and spectacles (a farmer tells me that his sheep are now fitted with dentures that prolong their useful life).

The marvels of modern medicine and surgery not only amaze but give me great encouragement. Labour-saving of all kinds makes old age easier – there is no need to light coal fires or cook over an open fire, and most people need not come down to cold rooms that need daily dusting and sweeping. It is undeniable that domestic and social conditions have improved tremendously for the vast majority during my lifetime. Unfortunately, in the general lifting of standards far too many people have been left behind, and in our prosperous community we have the disgrace of thousands of homeless and deprived people. It seems to me there is no excuse for policies which deliberately favour the able and well-off members of the community by robbing the vulnerable and least able of life's necessities. If I were young, I would be protesting vehemently against the greed and selfishness by which too many are hurt and neglected, without all the aids and benefits that I myself can enjoy. Whilst knitting and watching television, all I can do is try to encourage the church leaders and others who are in the thick of the struggle to improve things.

One morning in May there was a ring of my door bell and on the step stood a very big man unknown to me. For a split second I remembered all the warnings I had let go unheeded about answering doors to strangers. The man said with a note of enquiry, 'Mrs Hendry?' Yes. Then, 'I recognise you but you don't recognise me – John Monk.' John Monk? Up came the answer from my brain computer. Years ago a rather scruffy unpromising lad had come to the church in Shaw to join the Scouts. He had no father; his mother was a shy hardworking woman and it took all her time and energy to provide for John and herself. There was very little money to spare for Scouts or church or anything else. Now my visitor reminded me that I had made him a church member when he was 16. That was 34 years ago and we had not met since.

He asked about my daughters and old Scout friends. I asked him what he was doing now. He works in the Security Services in Papua, New Guinea, having emigrated after serving with the Lancashire Police Force. He was married and had a grown-up family. He had come for a month's holiday to England and was flying to Singapore the following day. He had made enquiries about my address, determined not to leave the country without seeing me and telling me how much the Shaw Church had meant to him and how he was now telling people here and in Papua, 'We had a woman minister 50 years ago – even though we lived in a small Lancashire town.' John Monk not only made my day but left me thinking how little the Church often knows of the good done for young people.

As Raymond Adams was still single-handed in the Purley church, he asked if I would conduct two weddings for him during the summer of '89. Imagine my surprise when he told me that the first bridegroom was the then world lightweight boxing champion, Duke Mackenzie. I had never met a prizefighter, and of course Duke and his fiancée Diane had to come and see me to make the arrangements for the wedding and rehearse the details of the service. When they arrived I could not think that the slim soft-spoken gentle-looking man could possibly be a fighter. On the day the bearing of the bridal party, their choice of hymns, the warmth of their families and friends, the heartiness of their singing, led experienced choir members to say the service was 'sheer magic'. That incident belied all I have ever thought about prizefighting, proving once again there is always a first time.

The second wedding was quite different but nearly as fascinating. Some years ago I had conducted the funeral of Mrs XY's husband. She was Greek – a beautiful granny with three daughters and a number of grandchildren, some of whom had an Iranian father. Her bridegroom was also Greek, a retired psychiatrist. Two older granddaughters were bridesmaids and the youngest, just two years old, was ready with her camera. That was another very happy occasion - and another new experience. I had never conducted a wedding before where grandchildren were teenage bridesmaids!

In August Joyce invited me to share a holiday with her in Wales. She had rented a delightful cottage 'far from the madding crowd'. On arrival we were warmly welcomed by the owners who lived in the same grounds and invited us one evening for dinner. Before going round, Joyce said she wanted to remain incognito as a doctor, as she did not want to get involved in a busman's holiday. I had no intention of saying what my profession had been. Over drinks, when asked where we had been in the area, it came out more or less accidentally that Clitheroe friends of mine had a cottage in the vicinity – and sure enough our host and hostess knew them. Then the man asked if I knew another Clitheroe resident? Yes, I did; I officiated at his brother's wedding. 'Oh,' exclaimed the host, 'so you are a registrar.' Taken aback, I had to confess and was overwhelmed with the response I got.

They had never met a woman minister and were thrilled to do so. As lapsed Anglicans they were saddened by their experience of the established Church, and the evening developed with many pleasant surprises and a highly interesting conversation in which Joyce also admitted to her own profession. As we talked about feminist theology I decided to lend them two books, one being the Prayer Fellowship Handbook by Kate Compston. Later they wrote to say the book had arrived just when there was a family crisis about a very sick child, and how helpful those prayers were. Joyce had come by that cottage on a computer. Does God still move in mysterious ways? And when does one retire from ministry?

1989 moved towards Christmas. John, frustrated by his physical limitations, decided that he could not endure another winter living in the spacious Chipstead house with its beautiful woodland views and, despite a depressed market, was able to negotiate with a builder to exchange Whytethorne for a new, more convenient house a short distance away. Consequently, after a chaotic two or three weeks, Christmas had to be celebrated in the unfinished muddle that was to be Kilderkin. Some of our family traditions survived – there was an Advent candle on the kitchen table and a big Christmas tree, surrounded by carefully-wrapped presents, in the hall. We had the usual food and drink, and my friend Dorothy and I were invited as always, but Sheena was missing as she was skiing in France until Boxing Day and more sadly 'Auntie Olive', who had shared Christmas with Joyce and John for many years, was not well enough to come. For the first time ever I missed the church celebrations, having succumbed to a chest infection.

I've often pondered on the hectic preparations for Christmas that most English people make even though they do not believe in the traditional Christian stories of Christmas. Sometimes at Christmas Eve Communion services I've commented that we could always count on the lapsed members and atheists being there. When I first married, Jim's family made little fuss about Christmas. My father-in-law's chemist shop did not close and there was no spending spree in Glasgow to compare with today's extravagant shopping in the south-east of England. We had a family party in Lancashire to which Jim's parents came until wartime restrictions made the gathering impossible. The Scots went wild about Hogmanay, the New Year, and Jim encouraged me to have New Year parties. Christmas did not seem so important.

In the Church latterly, I think nonconformists have become much more sensitive to the Advent season than they used to be, with the result that by Christmas morning sometimes it has seemed there's nothing more to say. In Clitheroe the one service on Christmas day was at 9.30 in the morning because, so it was said, by that time the children and parents had been awake hours, and to complete church duty by 10.30 left everybody free to get on with their own celebrations. The demand for traditional Christmas hymns and carols is still very strong and invariably there are murmurings if unknown new ones are introduced, but who today believes the theology of the popular old carols? And as carol concerts and nativity plays are multiplied at schools, at least some people get sick of singing by Christmas Day.

Once in Clitheroe I dared to set a plate of rice in the church vestibule with some Christian Aid reminders of the way 'the other half' lives, and met with caustic comments about spoiling people's happiness. Because my father was a minister, and Jim a doctor, I have never been away from home for Christmas and it has always been a busy working period; but it was a revelation to me to discover Purley's Christmas Day programme in the church and I still marvel at the sacrificial service given by a great many Purley church members. The day officially starts with a short service at ten in the morning and is followed by coffee, a full Christmas dinner, afternoon entertainment, a visit by Father Christmas and tea. This programme involves tremendous advance preparation in many kitchens, the provision of transport, the organisation of entertainment.

For many years it has been a real family party for lonely church people and for those unable to cook for a party. In addition social service workers have sent people newly released from prison, lonely immigrants, battered wives and children, elderly folk from Croydon bedsits and others in need. Sometimes it has been an impressive experience to see how such a varied group has become a family for while, and I have been filled with admiration for very affluent church members who have volunteered to leave their own luxury homes for several hours to wash up for a hundred and more in the church kitchen or to serve at table, when they could have been enjoying a happy time with family and friends. For ministers at Purley personal festivities have had to wait for Boxing Day, but when working I always found deep satisfaction at the end of Christmas Day.

One of the saddest sights I ever saw on Christmas Day occurred when I lived in Clitheroe. Joyce's mother-in-law and a widowed friend had gone to a luxury hotel on the Lancashire coast and they invited John, Joyce and me for the evening dinner party. The meal was excellent and competent staff slaved to provide gaiety for the guests, most of whom were apathetic or miserable. John's mother vowed that never again would she go away from home at Christmas!

So came 1990, the dawn of a new decade, and a thousand good wishes for the New Year together with forecasts galore. What could I look forward to: No more preaching? Declining physical and mental energy? Greater dependence on other people and less usefulness? Didn't John Wesley pray, 'Lord, never let me live to be useless?' I decided that 1990 must be the end of my autobiography. Nobody could persuade me that the reflections and reminiscences of an inactive retired minister could be worth writing or reading, so here begins the last chapter.

Sheena, with A-levels behind her and nine months to spend before university at Norwich in October, set off in January for an Israeli kibbutz where she was to work for four months. Not only was her absence a great loss for Joyce and John, but it was a sad break for me. From being a four-year-old when I came to Purley, Sheena had come regularly to my place most weeks and always she had been a ray of sunshine. I missed Bruce's schoolboy visits, but had got used to his being away from home; it made a serious gap in my routine when Sheena went away.

It is one of the penalties of longevity that people disappear from one's diary and as 1990 began I realised that this was beginning to happen for me. Some friends could not drive at night any more; one or two became ill or handicapped. My travelling companion, Mary, had to drop out of our programme because she required a hip operation. I myself felt no longer equal to driving miles to preach on Sunday mornings and less inclined to go to evening meetings. Life, I thought, was slowly getting more restricted, but what could I expect at my age? Wasn't I lucky to be well and mobile?

Some of my friends were actually saying they felt rejected or that they didn't feel they belonged any more. It is very easy in old age to indulge in self-pity, to complain of loneliness and to regret losing influence and responsibility for younger people. The role of parent with children somehow gets reversed: if we are fortunate we find ourselves cared for well by those for whom we once had all the responsibility. Some accept the experience more easily than others, but it must be very difficult indeed for old people who have been used to having power and authority and who lack family carers to submit to being looked after by strangers, no matter how competent and kind they may be; and I realise that a few of my friends have to accept such a situation. My own expectations at the beginning of 1990 were not exciting, but by March new possibilities began to surface. The Berlin Wall was down, and that meant that Sigrid and Wolfgang Steckel could come from Dessau to stay in June.

The routine of the early months of 1990 was uneventful. There were the usual church functions and many visitors came to see me, including old friends from Shaw. There was the occasional preaching engagement, and a number of invitations to local friends, all of which made life enjoyable to me but of no importance to anyone else. When I complained to Joyce that it grieved me I was not doing anything to help her she answered that the best thing I could do was to keep well and continue to be responsible for myself, and obviously that sounded very sensible. More than once on pastoral visits people have told me they couldn't see any purpose for them continuing to live, and I had tried to reassure them about the value of their lives to their families and neighbours and church, but it cannot be easy to accept a small walking on and off part on a stage after playing the lead. (Recently I have been fascinated to see some of my favourite actors and actresses continue in their profession in secondary roles, attractive and successful at a ripe old age.) If in 1990 churches continued to invite me to conduct services what ought I to do? I decided to judge every invitation if and when it arose – and that would mean writing very few new sermons.

No-one long in the ministry can have illusions about being listened to eagerly by everybody and quite often we preachers probably don't deserve keen attention. Yet I have to admit that I love writing sermons and I love preaching. Quite recently one of my fans paid me a compliment which ought to prevent conceit. She said, 'Kathleen, if you live to be 150 and go on preaching you can only get better!' For me new sermons mean new reading – and although I don't have to prepare new sermons every week, if I am without new theological reading I quickly feel I am starving.

One other aspect of ministry which gives me continuing satisfaction and I hope is useful to a few people is listening to individuals – sometimes on the phone, more often in person. I have plenty of time to give to people, old and young, and because of a very good relationship with Ray Adams, any counselling I do, he assures me, does not impinge on his ministry.

Wolfgang and Sigrid Steckel arrived in Purley in June 1990,

and we had a marvellous time together. Their impressions of life in south-east England, their hopes and fears for their own future, their naturalness and openness made for a great shared experience. Wolfgang preached a memorable sermon in Purley church, but it was a conversation at home which in an extraordinary way seemed to give me a fitting conclusion to this autobiography. He spoke of the Biblical Exodus and his country and commented, 'We have escaped, we are free and like the Israelites, we are bewildered, we are afraid - we cannot guess the future.' I suddenly remembered that first sermon I wrote on the text from Exodus 14, 'Fear not, stand still and see the salvation of the Lord.' Newer versions translate 'stand firm'.

All through the years I have failed to answer the question Why? and have grown to accept my ignorance and the mystery of life, but today I know that the initial faith put into that first inadequate and naive sermon endures. Like the East Germans on the threshold of new experience, I admit to doubts and fears and bewilderment. Often I cannot see light at the end of the tunnel, yet looking back I know that goodness and mercy have followed me so far, and I surrender to no-one my confidence in God's love and guidance. In the changed and changing world of the '90s there is much that makes me ashamed of my generation. The unspeakable tragedy of war and injustice, of cruelty and poverty, linger on; but when I look at the younger generation with their skills and confidence, their ability to make friends and their knowledge of the world, hope leaps up. God never leaves himself without a witness.